Pages from
the Life
of
Dmitri
Shostakovich

Pages from the Life of Dmitri Shostakovich

by Dmitri & Ludmilla Sollertinsky

TRANSLATED BY GRAHAM HOBBS
& CHARLES MIDGLEY

Harcourt Brace Jovanovich
New York and London

Printed in the United States of America

Library of Congress Cataloging in Publication Data

Sollertinsky, Dmitri.
Pages from the life of Dmitri Shostakovich.
Translation of Stranitsy zhizni Dmitriia
Shostakovicha.
Includes index.
1. Shostakovich, Dmitrii Dmitrievich, 1906–1975.
2. Composers—Russia—Biography. D. Sollertinsky,
Ludmilla, joint author. II. Title.
ML410.S53S643   785′.092′4 [B]   79-3364
ISBN 0-15-170730-8

Set in Linotype Granjon

First edition

B C D E

[Contents]

ILLUSTRATIONS

[Authors' Note]

In August 1975 Dmitri Shostakovich, the composer, died.
Mankind had lost one of its greatest creative musical spirits.

A good deal has been written about Shostakovich, mostly
studies of his work, but some popular books as well. Our
book offers the reader an outline of the life of this great figure
in twentieth-century music. Those episodes which, as chance
would have it, we have managed to learn about in detail, we
portray in detail: they include his last years, his friendship
with Ivan Sollertinsky, and his relationships with his students.

Apart from the large number of published sources—
Shostakovich's autobiography, other people's reminiscences
of him, and his letters—we have drawn extensively on material from our archives: the composer's letters to Ivan Sollertinsky and to Olga and Dmitri Sollertinsky; other works
from his hand; Ivan Sollertinsky's notebooks; materials from
the Shostakovich archives, to which we were given access by
Shostakovich's wife, Irina; her recollections and those of his
children; and reminiscences by his sister Zoya and nephew
Dmitri Frederiks. To all the above, and to Shostakovich's
friends and students who shared their memories and archives
with us, we extend our deep gratitude for their invaluable
help.

Pages from
the Life
of
Dmitri
Shostakovich

[1906–1922]

St. Petersburg at the beginning of the twentieth century: on either side of a broad, straight ribbon of a gravel-covered boulevard stand tall, smart buildings and here and there a handsome mansion. The rows of elegant façades are occasionally interrupted by a square with a monument surrounded by a little garden, or a bridge decorated with groups of sculptures, or the broad colonnade of a magnificent cathedral.

This is Nevsky Prospekt. A little boy in a sailor suit often walks here, accompanied by his aunt Alexandra and his two sisters—Maria, the elder, and baby Zoya. The boy lives not far from the Nikolaevsky Station, near Nevsky Prospekt on Nikolaevsky Street, which is straight and regular with two rows of almost identical houses. Nevsky Prospekt—resplendent in summer, but stern and gloomy on winter evenings—is one of his first memories.

Another of his memories is of a typical evening at home in the drawing room. Some friends have come to see his parents. After tea, as always, the music-making begins. His mother, Sofia Vasilyevna, sits down at the grand piano. Their neighbor, Boris Sass-Tesovsky, an engineer and quite a good amateur cellist, tunes his instrument and picks up his bow. Sometimes one of the visitors happens to play the violin, and then his mother gets out some of her favorite music—a trio by Tchaikovsky or Rachmaninov. His father, on the other hand, loves singing and performs old Russian romances with real feeling, accompanying himself on the guitar.

His mother played well. She had studied at the Conservatory and once thought of becoming a professional pianist, teaching and perhaps doing some concert work—not in St. Petersburg, of course, since she was not talented enough for that, but in a town in the provinces. Shortly before finishing at the Conservatory, however, she met a young chemist and engineer named Dmitri Boleslavovich Shostakovich, who had graduated from St. Petersburg University; in 1902 she married him and gave herself up entirely to her family. Their daughter Maria was born in 1903, then Dmitri in 1906, and three years later their daughter Zoya.

Dmitri Boleslavovich worked at the Central Department of Weights and Measures under Mendeleev, the famous chemist who had founded it and who had devised the periodic table of the elements. Following Mendeleev's death he went to work at the Ministry of Trade and Industry. He was a good engineer, a capable organizer, a man content with life. He was observant, alert, and inquisitive, and did not confine his interests to his job, but spent his spare time working selflessly on a committee to help the coastal dwellers of the Russian North, and with a society to assist Siberian students at St. Petersburg University.

The Shostakoviches were an ordinary family of the Russian intelligentsia who liked to celebrate birthdays and saints' days with presents and treats, and who saw the New Year in with great ceremony. On Sundays the whole family would go to the theater, visit friends, or have company at home. They often entertained visitors, and when they did there would generally be music. On such evenings little Dmitri would do everything he could to stay in the drawing room as long as possible. He could not be taken off at bedtime without a terrible scene. Usually he tried to hide in some out-of-the-way corner in the naive hope that he would be forgotten and left in peace to enjoy the music.

But it was not only the sounds of the drawing room and the opera house, where the children were often taken for a matinée performance, which made up his earliest musical impressions. He listened eagerly to all the many and varied sounds around him: the nanny gently singing a simple tune as she put the children to bed; the sounds he heard during their walks, spilling out of the cinemas which had recently opened on Nevsky Prospekt—sounds that were first happy, then sad, rushing headlong one moment then slow and tender the next. And there was the grand, awesome sound of the choir in the handsome church with the colored-tile exterior—Trinity Church, near their home.

The courtyard of the house itself provided a good many things to listen to. Late in the St. Petersburg spring when the sun began to shine more warmly and the windows, sealed shut throughout the winter, were flung wide open, a most interesting collection of people gathered in the yard. The cranberry seller, a sprightly old woman in a bright shawl, would cry piercingly to an intricate rhythm, "Cranberries, cranberries, fresh from the snow!" Before long the girl from the nearest pastry shop would take over: "Fresh pies, fancy buns!" The hurdy-gurdy man was also a frequent visitor: when he began to turn the handle on his brightly painted box, the entire yard would be deafened with strident, off-key polkas and waltzes. These memories of his childhood remained with Shostakovich all his life. More than that, they bore fruit ten and even forty years later.

When the elder daughter, Maria, reached the age of ten, her mother began to give her music lessons. Her small brother was generally not far away. He listened intently to the pieces she was studying and to his mother's comments, looking at the music in front of Maria and remembering how she held her hands over the keys.

He expressed no desire to take lessons himself, and no one

suggested it. His mother held the view that music lessons too early did nothing but harm: "I don't altogether approve of people who torment a gifted child simply in order to create a sensation by pushing a scared little creature out onto a concert stage and giving it the awesome title of a 'prodigy.' It's most unusual, in my view, for such a child to develop later into anything really interesting. For the most part, they cause a stir at the age of five or six because of their precocious abilities, but at thirty they seem perfectly ordinary; their creative powers have dried up, their system is drained and they are burnt out before their time."

True to her convictions, Mrs. Shostakovich sat her son down at the piano only in the summer of 1915, shortly before his ninth birthday. At that time, of course, she had no idea of the musical career that lay before him; she imagined him going into engineering like his father. As a result, his parents did not even send him to a high school, where he would have received an education in the humanities; instead, he went to the College of Commerce, where the emphasis was on the exact sciences and accounting. In fact, he received music lessons only because it was the custom among the intelligentsia. It was generally accepted that, whatever his profession, an educated man should be able to sight-read simple pieces, accompany a singer, or play music for dancing if asked, when among company.

But on the day of his first lesson—quite literally, during the first few minutes of his studies—Mrs. Shostakovich realized that her son had phenomenal musical ability. To begin with, he announced that he did not wish to learn about the "little lines," as his sister had done at her first lessons; he wanted a piece to play. His mother, smiling to herself, decided to dampen his ardor by setting an arrangement of an andante from a Haydn symphony on the music stand. Although not technically difficult, the piece required a knowl-

edge of musical notation and at least a little keyboard training.

Mrs. Shostakovich thought the boy would be put off. Instead, he merely asked her to explain what the sharps, flats,
and naturals meant (he had long since committed to memory
what note lay on what line, as a result of watching his sister's
lessons), and then, frowning with concentration, he began to
play slowly but with absolute accuracy, compensating
quaintly for his lack of familiarity with the keyboard by
means of fingerings that he made up as he went along. After
one or two lessons he could already play the whole of
Tchaikovsky's *Children's Album* with ease.

Mrs. Shostakovich soon became aware that her teaching
skills were not adequate to working with so gifted a pupil.
She decided to send her son to one of the best teachers in St.
Petersburg, Ignati Glyasser, with whom her elder daughter
was already studying. Maria was making significant progress,
but did not stand out among the other pupils in her class.
Consequently, Glyasser reacted somewhat ironically when
Mrs. Shostakovich presented her son to him, saying proudly,
"I'm bringing you a remarkable pupil!" "All mothers have
remarkable children," he replied with a smile. But once he
had heard the boy play he readily admitted that Mrs. Shostakovich might be right.

Young Dmitri began to attend his classes. Glyasser, once a
pupil of the well-known German pianists Kullak and Klind-
worth, imparted to his pupils a fine technique with enviable
nimbleness of the fingers and a sure, firm touch. He evidently
paid too little attention, however, to the artistic side of piano
playing. He was an excellent technician at the piano but not a
great musician, being inclined to dryness and an unfeelingly
rational approach. For the sensitive young Shostakovich,
who was developing at an astonishing rate, it became increasingly difficult to find a common language with his teacher.

Shostakovich was also greatly attracted to composing. He loved to feel something personal, something never before heard, grow beneath his fingers. The boy lived music. It ceased to be just a pleasure for him, it became a necessity. He needed music to express himself, his feelings, his still very immature and often childish ideas.

Glyasser could not understand this. He felt composition distracted his pupil from the main task at hand, which was to develop a good piano technique. He even tried to make the boy give up composing. The result he achieved was completely different: as Shostakovich laconically recalled at a later date, studying with Glyasser "got boring." Realizing this, Mrs. Shostakovich turned to another teacher, Professor Rozanova of the Conservatory, with whom she herself had taken lessons.

The lessons with Rozanova were a success. Her approach was strikingly different from Glyasser's. She worked patiently, without losing her temper or making young Dmitri work on endless technical exercises; instead, she concentrated on different kinds of touch and the mood of a piece. With her he learned to listen to music with the meticulous sensitivity of a poet. Rozanova also encouraged his experiments in composition and felt that he should pursue them seriously with a teacher.

Those were stormy, anxious years. First there was World War I, with bad news from the front and persistent rumors of betrayal and treason "at the highest levels" within the Tsar's family. Then came popular uprisings: demonstrations in the streets dispersed by mounted police, sounds of shooting, and columns of workers marching down Nevsky Prospekt almost in front of where the Shostakoviches lived. Once, during a clash with some workers, a policeman killed a boy before young Dmitri's very eyes.

Shostakovich was a witness to the February Revolution that overthrew the Tsarist government. And in April 1917, when Lenin returned from abroad to St. Petersburg and thousands of workers went to greet him at the Station, Dmitri too was there. He and his classmates from the College of Commerce on Shpalerny Street, a stone's throw from the Liteiny Bridge, joined the column of workers crossing the bridge over the Neva toward the square that today bears Lenin's name. He could not hear what Lenin said because he had to stand a long way off on the edge of the square, above which rose a relentless clamor of voices. But the spectacle of a billowing sea of people, the elemental force of the events taking place, and the figure of Lenin—all this was imprinted forever in his memory, to pour out later in sweeping symphonic canvases. Even at that time, in 1917, he composed the children's pieces *The Soldier, Hymn of Freedom,* and *Funeral March for the Victims of the Revolution.* He had written other things as well. At the age of ten and eleven, young Dmitri was not interested solely in the historic events which were taking place. He wrote an opera called *Tsygany* (The Gypsies) after the poem by Pushkin; a ballet called *Rusalochka* (The Mermaid) based on a story by Andersen; a trilogy for piano entitled *In the Forest*; a fantasy for two pianos and other piano pieces.

He also found time for other hobbies. A quiet, intense, introspective child, he never liked rowdy boys' games with lots of shouting and running about. While still very young, he would play for hours building improbable structures with his blocks. Later he became thoughtful and aloof, withdrawing into his reflections and forgetting about everything else. Then the time came when he grew passionately fond of books. At first he read ordinary children's books—fairy tales and stories about animals. Then he was drawn to books on famous people and outstanding events. Finally it was Gogol, Leskov,

9

Chekhov, and Dostoevsky—authors he would love all his life.

Even in his early teens, however, Dmitri looked on his favorite authors from an active and creative point of view. The images which captured his attention begged to be re-created in musical terms. Early in 1918, in a letter to his favorite aunt—his mother's sister, Nadezhda Kokoulina—he wrote: "I've decided to set Lermontov's poem about Tsar Vasilyevich, the young guardsman, and the fearless merchant Kalashnikov to music. At the moment I'm writing music for Gogol's *Dreadful Revenge*."

From the age of about eight on, young Dmitri had also enjoyed writing poetry. All her life his mother treasured a tiny homemade postcard on which he had written in a childish hand:

> I'm sending you a new poem:
>
> Morning peeps through the window,
> The sun is already up.
> The window is bright with a golden light,
> The sun's playing games with the pup.

Amusing, naive, and childish, but proof of an enduring interest. "A new poem" implies that there had been earlier attempts; further efforts would follow. The envelope containing his letter to his aunt also held two long poems: *The Two Bears* and *A Proverb*. The young author viewed them critically: "The rhymes are a bit strained. *The Two Bears* isn't right, but *A Proverb* is better."

About that time his years of study at the College of Commerce came to an end. His teachers, his parents, and he himself had all realized that he was not in the least interested in a career in engineering, let alone commerce. At a family conference in the summer of 1917 it was decided that the boy should be sent to the famous high school founded by the well-known teacher Maria Stoyunina, a friend of the Dostoevsky family. The school owed its reputation to its brilliant teaching staff, many of whom were university professors, and to the high standards it set for its pupils. The school's upper-intelligentsia atmosphere helped to bring out the pupils' individual aptitudes and develop their abilities.

Concerts were given regularly, at least once a month, in the school hall, where guest musicians and Conservatory students took part, and children at the school also performed. At these concerts Dmitri Shostakovich played music by Schumann, Chopin, and Grieg. He was a good pupil, especially in the arts. He could present his thoughts in a clear, orderly, terse, precise manner, and was renowned for his individual and often paradoxical wit and his wonderful sense of humor. His teachers believed that he might make a scholar of note.

Dmitri was very fond of animals. He would play happily with the dogs at the family's dacha in the country, and took touching care of newly hatched birds fallen from their nests. This love of living creatures, "our little brothers," remained with the composer all his life. He always kept dogs and cats, and tried to take vacations where he could be close to animals.

As time went by, Dmitri's parents began to see more clearly that their son's future lay in music. His playing developed a maturity and originality beyond his years. Whenever the family was invited out or had company, Dmitri would be asked to play some Grieg, Chopin, or occasionally something of his own. Perhaps it was his own pieces which most impressed his listeners. A brief description has come down to us from Konstantin Fedin, then still starting out in the world of letters, on whom the young musician made an indelible impression:

It was wonderful to be among the guests when the bony boy with thin lips pressed together, a small, narrow, faintly Roman nose, and old-fashioned spectacles with bright metal frames . . . entered the large room and, rising on tiptoe, sat down at the huge piano. Wonderful, for by some obscure law of contradictions the bony boy was transformed at the piano into a bold musician with a man's strength in his fingers and an arresting rhythmic drive. He played his own compositions, which were full of the influences of the new music—unexpected works which forced one to listen as if one were in the theater, where everything is so clear that one must laugh or weep. His music talked, chattered, was sometimes quite outspoken. Among confused dissonances it suddenly revealed such melodies that all eyebrows were raised. Then the boy got up and went quietly to join his mother, who blushed and smiled as if the applause were for her and not her wordless son. Later, when the musician was beset from all sides with requests to play again and he just sat there, eyes lowered angrily behind his spectacles, hands on his sharp boyish knees, his mother said, "Well go on, Dmitri, play something else."

In an instant Dmitri obediently stood up and walked with a child's awkwardness to the piano. As he touched the keys he briskly regained his manly stature and took on the purposefulness without which great music is inconceivable. Those with a gift for prediction could already see in the web of his singular imaginings the future Dmitri Shostakovich.

This description refers to one of the soirées held at the home of the eminent St. Petersburg surgeon Ivan Grekov, where the cream of the capital's intelligentsia gathered. Regular visitors included the writer Alexei Tolstoy, a large, stout, benevolent-looking Russian nobleman, and his exact opposite, Alexei Remizov, a short, broken man who wrote of mystical and diabolic things, and himself resembled the Devil of popular imagination. The eminent director and theatrical personality Vladimir Nemirovich-Danchenko would appear there whenever he came up from Moscow. The poetess Anna Akhmatova would be there, listening kindly to the praises lavished on her, and Grekov's medical colleagues gladly came to forget their professional concerns. The young bass Pavel Andreev, later a soloist at the Kirov Theater, and the pianist Vladimir Sofronitsky, one of the finest interpreters of Scriabin, appeared at these improvised soirées just for the honor of attending.

Possibly the most esteemed among Grekov's guests was Alexander Glazounov. A major Russian composer and the younger contemporary, pupil, and friend of Rimsky-Korsakov, he was an undisputed authority in musical circles. He had heard Dmitri several times at the Grekovs', and had been interested in this uncommonly gifted boy for some time. It was to him that Mrs. Shostakovich turned for advice. "Having satisfied himself as to Dmitri's knowledge and abilities," she later recalled, "Glazounov decided that he could easily go straight into the composition department and omit all the theoretical courses. He said something to me then that I wrote down and that remains among my most precious memories: 'I cannot recall a time when there were children as gifted as your son at the Conservatory.'"

Dmitri took the entrance examination in the fall of 1919. For many years now the Conservatory has been an institute of higher education attended by young men and women of between seventeen and twenty after completing their secondary education. But things were different in 1919: to get into the Conservatory, it was necessary only to have a certain degree of talent, a knowledge of musical discipline, and the ability to work like a professional. Bearded young men with degrees in engineering or medicine and girls in pig-tails frequently sat next to one another in class. One year, for example, a military engineer named Nikolai Miaskovsky, who was almost thirty, studied in the same class as a phenomenally gifted ten-year-old named Sergei Prokofiev.

At the entrance examination, therefore, the bony Shostakovich, looking even younger than his thirteen years, found himself in the company of students far older than he. The examination went easily: he played a number of his compositions, answered questions testing his ear and his theoretical knowledge, and then was allowed to go. A few hours later the word had spread through the enormous building on Teatralny Square: the Conservatory had accepted a student whose talents were, as Glazounov put it, "on a level with Mozart's."

Those were very difficult years for Russia and for revolutionary Petrograd. The country lay in ruins, a prey to savage famine, ravaged by the many years of war and the ensuing foreign intervention. Ration cards were introduced, but not much could be obtained with them: millet, vegetable oil, an occasional sardine. There was no butter, sugar, or meat in the city. Fuel was short. Instead of their traditional Russian or Dutch stoves, which needed a large amount of firewood, people used tiny cast-iron ones which for some reason were known as *bourzhouiki*. They could be stoked up with a handful of shavings but did not stay hot for long—just enough to boil a kettle or heat up some thin millet soup.

City transport was not functioning well; the streetcars rarely ran. People who needed to get to the other side of the enormous city, which spread out along both banks and the many branches of the Neva, would ride on the steps of the cars, hanging on by their fingernails. Every day Dmitri had to go a substantial distance from his house near the Moscow Station to Teatralny Square, where the Leningrad Conservatory still stands today. In all weather, every day he covered that distance both ways on foot, and every day without fail he appeared at his classes.

The Conservatory had admitted him to two faculties at the same time—composition and piano. He continued to study the piano with Rozanova, and for composition went to Rimsky-Korsakov's relative and favorite pupil, Maximilian Steinberg. Steinberg was a marvelous teacher, a brilliant professional who could also instill a high degree of professionalism in his pupils. He was very conscientious. In spite of the cold (the Conservatory too was without heat), he always arrived in the classroom punctually and was painstaking in his work with his students. It cannot be said that they treated him in like manner, for the cold, the prospect of working on an empty stomach, and the long distances put many of them off. While Steinberg's regular class was full in the fall, by the spring very few students still came to it, but among those few invariably was Dmitri.

The classes proved most interesting. Besides academic disciplines and practical composition, Steinberg attached great importance to general musical development. His classes always did a lot of four-hand playing, and then analyzed the form of the pieces played and the way they were arranged for the instruments. Steinberg explained everything to do with the harmony clearly and concisely, drawing his pupils' attention to interesting passages and nurturing their harmonic taste.

Dmitri's fellow classmates were struck by how quickly and completely he picked up and assimilated anything related to the music. The principles of harmonization, the peculiarities of modulation and texture, the logic of counterpoint, the twists of harmony, rhythm, and timbre—in all this he was entirely at home. In aural tests he could take down the most complicated passages from dictation quickly and without a mistake. His ear, in the sensitivity and accuracy with which it identified sounds, was like a piece of sophisticated acoustical equipment, and his musical memory instantly captured what he heard. Indeed, this capacity of his so delighted his comrades that they went out of their way to devise more and more new tests for him. Apparently his ear for music was not only absolute, which in itself is important for a musician, but also internal—that is, visual or conceptual—since it did not depend on what he heard; he could pick up the tiniest details of the music just from looking at the pages of a piano reduction or score. He could sight-read any piece with ease, no matter how difficult, as well as orchestral scores with a large number of transposed parts. In the spring and fall, when the temperature in the Conservatory's classrooms permitted music-making, he constantly played arrangements of symphonic and chamber works.

Dmitri had other tutors besides Steinberg in the composition faculty. He studied polyphony with Professor Nikolai Sokolov, a gifted composer and teacher who also had uncommon literary talents. On the exterior Sokolov looked stern and forbidding, but in fact he was great fun and a witty, inexhaustibly inventive storyteller. His classes always combined hard work with anecdotes, jokes, and pranks. Sokolov's harmonic and polyphonic technique was superb, and he could correct exercises quickly and well, putting his pupils on the right track. He lived close to the Conservatory in Maximilianovsky Passage but, unlike the punctilious Steinberg, often skipped lessons. This did not worry the other students unduly, for they too were glad to get out of a lesson. Dmitri, however, found a way to outsmart his teacher: not finding him in the classroom, he would seek him out at his home. In this way he managed to acquire a fine, solidly based body of knowledge. After Sokolov's death in 1922 Dmitri completed the course in polyphony under Steinberg, with whom he also studied form and orchestration.

For music history Dmitri went to the lectures given by Alexander Ossovsky, first a professor and later, in 1922, rector of the Conservatory, who gave clear and accurate descriptions of historical periods, and related musical developments to the overall cultural and political background.

Soon Dmitri, the youngest of the composition students, was the center of attention throughout the faculty. The Conservatory had a young composers' club: meetings were normally held in the Conservatory canteen, and professors and even Glazounov himself would look in. There would be a lot of playing followed by animated discussions of the pieces. The subject of the discussion often proved to be a new work by Shostakovich. He took along his piano preludes and his first orchestral composition, a scherzo dedicated to his teacher, Maximilian Steinberg; later he played the *Fantastic Dances* for piano and the Theme and Variations for Orchestra dedicated to the memory of Professor Sokolov. (Almost all the compositions dating from his childhood and youth are dedicated to someone—a teacher, a friend, or a relative. It appears that the young musician shared the treasures of his heart and imagination generously with those dear to him.)

As far as composition was concerned, then, everything was fine. Things were more difficult with the piano.

At first he was happy studying with Rozanova. He had grown accustomed to her methods and was attached to her as a person. By the end of his first year at the Conservatory, however, it had become plain to him that he must change teachers. Rozanova's essentially feminine, refined, and delicate but restricted piano style was too oppressive for a musician with his phenomenal talents. After agonies of doubt as to whether it was ethical, Dmitri eventually made the decision. In his second year he was taking lessons from another professor, Leonid Nikolaev.

Nikolaev was the most popular teacher in the piano faculty. Maria Yudina and Vladimir Sofronitsky, both first-rate musicians, studied with him. Every pianist tried to get into his classes, but he accepted very few; of course he agreed to take Dmitri without hesitation.

Nikolaev ran his classes his own way. He did not give lessons to one pupil at a time; everybody who wished to come, came. Many, knowing what was to be played, brought the music with them so as to understand better and remember his comments. The atmosphere in the classroom was like a concert hall. No one even considered leaving during a lesson (and not only when someone was playing). Latecomers (they were very rare) stood timidly in the small area between the two sets of doors dividing the classroom from the corridor, their ears to the narrow crack between the inner doors.

The "chosen few" whose turn it was to play met in the classroom an hour before Nikolaev arrived. They checked with one another to see if they had remembered his instructions correctly, and would all but fight for the chance to play for a few minutes before the lesson began. Both grand pianos would be going at once, each playing something different and each player trying to outplay the other in order to hear himself better. This improbable concert continued until a student posted by the professors' cloakroom ran in crying, "He's here!" Everyone rushed to sit in the deep oilcloth chairs and go over their music. Nikolaev entered, spruce, elegant, and amiable, and the lesson began.

At the start it was so cold in the classroom that they played in coats, boots, and gloves with no fingers. At first their fingers froze on touching the icy keys and could hardly move, but gradually the students warmed up and their playing became more fluid and fluent. It was better when the *bourzhouiki* arrived. The students brought fuel—one a log, another a plank from a cupboard, the leg of a chair, or a section of picture frame. The next one to play sat by the little stove and warmed his hands. When he went to the piano, the following pupil took his place.

Students brought pieces they already knew well and had worked on all they could by themselves. Nikolaev listened from start to finish, never interrupting to comment. When the piece was over he would generally say, "Very nice." Then the work began, and when he had finished, nothing as a rule remained of the "very nice" performance. Nikolaev sought to make his pupils listen intently to the music and find meaning in every bar, every note. He drew their attention to the piece's texture, to its harmonic and rhythmic features, the way the melody developed, the construction of the cadences and how they were reached. He analyzed all these details.

Sometimes, having finished a set piece, Dmitri would show Nikolaev his compositions. Nikolaev was himself a composer, having written a number of works which enjoyed some limited success in their time. They were logical, perfect in form, and very pleasant to listen to. Unfortunately, they had no individuality or life of their own. Nikolaev, a fine and sensitive musician, was well aware of this and, hard as it was for him to endure the disparity between his professional ability and his creative powers, he found the strength to give up composing and devote himself entirely to piano playing and teaching. But for that very reason—as one who could feel the music "from the inside," from the point of view of a creator rather than a mere listener—he was able to give Dmitri truly valuable advice, making penetrating and sensitive comments on what he heard. The boy valued these comments highly. Much later, reminiscing about his years at the Conservatory, he regretted that Nikolaev had not given a special course in composition.

Glazounov kept a careful watch over the rapid development of this brilliant young man. He always took a paternal interest in the students and was invariably present at all the examinations held at the Conservatory for musicians of different specializations. For all his busy timetable, he never tired of listening to pianists, violinists, cellists, singers, and wind and brass players. After everything he listened to, he would jot down a short comment on a piece of paper. His comments concerning Shostakovich have survived.

In the spring of 1920, at the end of Dmitri's first year of studies: "Outstandingly gifted as a musician and virtuoso. Presentation already highly individual and mature."

1921: "An excellent musician despite his young age. Such early development is remarkable."

1922: ". . . a musician with talents quite out of the ordinary and a technique advanced beyond his years. . . . thoughtful presentation, full of atmosphere." And of his development as a composer: "Exceptional gifts which have blossomed early. Something to be astonished and delighted at. Fine technical workmanship, interesting and original content. (5$^+$)"*

A year later, without waiting for him to conclude his term at the Conservatory, Glazounov was calling Dmitri "already a completely mature musician."

Glazounov's interest showed in more than just his comments and enthusiastic acclaim for a brilliantly unfolding talent. He did everything in his power to ensure that during those difficult years of meager rations and severe restrictions, when clothing and food were constantly in short supply, Dmitri got what he required. The young boy needed to develop physically at a time when the burdens he carried—both the mental ones associated with his rapid development and incessant absorption of knowledge, and physical ones, too (a pianist's life also involves hard physical work)—were almost too much for his frail body.

* 5 is the highest mark awarded under the system used in the Soviet Union.—Trans.

Glazounov arranged for Dmitri to receive a grant from the Borodin Fund, which was financed by receipts from performances of Borodin's opera *Prince Igor*. Under a covenant by Borodin's friends, who had completed the opera and succeeded in getting it staged, the money due them under copyright went into the fund to help talented student composers. Glazounov also applied for special academic rations of sugar, butter, and meat to be issued to Dmitri.

In 1921, recognizing that even this was not enough, Glazounov wrote a letter to the People's Commissar for Education, Anatoly Lunacharsky, under whose authority the Conservatory operated at that time:

> Most Esteemed Sir,
>
> In the St. Petersburg State Conservatory there is a highly gifted pupil named Dmitri Shostakovich who will undoubtedly become a composer, and who is taking classes in the theory of composition and the pianoforte. He is making phenomenal progress but this, unfortunately, is having a deleterious effect on his frail health, which has been weakened by lack of nourishment.
>
> I humbly request you to support my plea that this most talented boy be provided with nourishment in order to increase his strength.

When Dmitri fell ill two years later, Glazounov again appealed to Lunacharsky for help. This time his letter closed with the words: "The death of such a man would be an irremediable loss for the arts the world over."

The most remarkable thing is that there was no creative affinity between the venerable musician and his young charge. Indeed, it would be difficult to imagine two more strikingly different artists. Their music was as different as they themselves differed physically from each other: Glazounov massive, impressive, rather corpulent, deliberate, and phlegmatic, reminiscent of a khan; and Shostakovich, all sharp corners, tense, bright, and unkempt like a sparrow. Glazounov's music was balanced, classically beautiful, and forthright, whereas his young contemporary's was already angular, sometimes dramatic and sometimes sarcastic, but never restful, as if gatherering into itself all the storms and passions of its age. This music, novel in every way, was foreign to Glazounov, yet he was well aware of the talents possessed by the young student.

For a while Dmitri continued to go to school while studying in two faculties at the Conservatory. True, the Conservatory offered classes in general subjects for the few pupils who, like him, had not yet completed their secondary education, but the standard of teaching was generally poor, attention being devoted mainly to the specialized disciplines. His parents resolved that he would not take the easy way out: their son must not only have a secure grounding in music, but become a genuinely cultivated person, well informed in many subjects.

So Dmitri, like both his sisters, continued to go to the old Stoyunina High School. Everyone quickly realized, however, that this double life made impossible demands on the still immature and growing boy. Professor Afanasyev, the director of the high school, asked Dmitri's father to come for a talk. His view was that, since Dmitri had firmly decided on a future as a musician, it was nonsensical and even dangerous to make him study in a school with exacting requirements and a broad curriculum designed for future scientists. This conversation hastened a long overdue decision: Dmitri was transferred to another school with a normal curriculum—a school that, in addition, was very close to his home on Kuznetsky Lane.

Now Dmitri had more time for music and knew how to use

it to best advantage; his thirst for knowledge and new musical experiences was insatiable. After a full day of study, in the evening, he would rush off to the Philharmonic Hall, the Opera, or simply visit friends and make music. "We students were forever going to performances at the Philharmonic, the chapel, or the Opera," the composer recalled later. "We always attended the rehearsals. Having no money, we turned sneaking into the hall free but without creating a scene into a fine art—maintaining appearances but driving the ticket office and the theater administration to distraction. But these little misdeeds were completely justified by the range of musical knowledge we acquired by such undesirable means."

In spite of the hardships of that period, the theatrical and concert life of St. Petersburg was full and varied. The opera houses presented the best productions of the world repertoire —operas by Verdi and Tchaikovsky, Wagner and Rimsky-Korsakov, Gluck, Mozart, Weber, and Glinka—with the wonderful actor-singers Fyodor Chaliapin and Ivan Yershov performing. Music by nineteenth-century Russian composers and the Viennese masters, and by Brahms, Wagner, and Berlioz could be heard almost every day in the Philharmonic Hall.

But active music-making predominated markedly over passive acquaintance. The young people at the Conservatory would often meet at someone's house to play an unfamiliar piece as a piano duet. Such was their enthusiasm that they were prepared to walk miles and go without supper into the bargain.

On Monday evenings they usually gathered at the home of a well-known music lover, Anna Vogt. Musicians filled the large room, which was divided by an arch with marble columns. Composers, conductors, and pianists would be there, as well as professors and students from the Conservatory.

The program for the evening was never announced in advance, but everyone waited impatiently for Monday to come round. People played their own compositions—pieces they had just completed, or sometimes even unfinished works; they were keen to share their ideas and hear constructive and informed criticism. At Vogt's they also encountered modern music from abroad: works by Alban Berg and Arnold Schönberg, the French group "Les Six," and Hindemith, and new pieces by Igor Stravinsky.

But Dmitri's interests extended beyond just music. He was keenly interested in ballet and enjoyed going to the cinema, where the first Soviet pictures by Pudovkin, Eisenstein, and other fine directors were showing. He saw films with such well-known stars as Emil Jannings, Konrad Veidt, Priscilla Din, and Asta Nielsen. He read a great deal, too, and being interested in painting, was friendly with students at the Academy of Arts. Like other Conservatory students, he was often to be seen in the handsome Academy building on the bank of the Neva, and not only at exhibitions, since there were often evening events as well. The Academy students would put on plays they had written themselves, providing their own scenery, for which the students at the Conservatory composed music.

All in all, Dmitri achieved a surprising amount. With him, time seemed to stretch and accommodate an unheard-of number of activities—a characteristic that would remain with him all his life. It clearly reflects the influence of his family and the habits acquired through his upbringing by his mother in accordance with strict pedagogical principles.

Though enormously busy with two Conservatory faculties, studies at school, and his extensive musical interests and contacts, Dmitri still had time for a wide circle of friends. As in the past, his family often went visiting and constantly received guests at home. Family celebrations were particularly enjoyable; a relaxed and merry mood prevailed. Maria, vivacious yet gentle, feminine and attractive, and Zoya, a strange, provocative schoolgirl with an angular and uncompromising character, contrasted with the serious, sometimes distant Dmitri, who seemed to hide behind his shining spectacles. But he too could be mischievous at times, surprising people with his not always unimpeachable humor.

Dmitri's father was the life and soul of the party, but the guiding force behind it was undoubtedly the intelligent, strong-willed, diplomatic, and impeccably well-bred Mrs. Shostakovich. They ate in the dining room, which was so narrow that the laden table, at which the guests sat almost shoulder to shoulder, seemed to take up all the space. Then they went into the drawing room. Mrs. Shostakovich—small but very erect, seeing everything with her piercing blue eyes —led the conversation and made sure that everyone felt at ease. Mr. Shostakovich, of medium height and a bit portly, joined one or another of the groups in the room, smiling a welcome. There was music and they played charades. The acting was full of humor and quirky details, and was accompanied by witty musical improvisations. Dmitri sat at the piano, a mischievous gleam in his eyes. All present were genuinely happy.

[1922–1926]

February 1922 brought great grief to the Shostakovich family when Dmitri's father died at the age of forty-six. It was a terrible and unexpected blow. Young Dmitri's life had been going smoothly at its accustomed, if hectic, pace; the future had seemed bright and secure. Then in the course of a few days everything changed. His father caught a cold, and the cold developed into double pneumonia.

The doctors did all they could, but early in the century when there were still no antibiotics or sulfonilamides, that was not much. Professor Grekov visited the patient regularly and during the critical period did not leave his bedside all night. But the patient could not be saved. Early in the morning of February 24 Mrs. Shostakovich, drawn, gray hairs showing at her temples, came out of the bedroom and told the children, "Father is no longer with us."

"I remember the funeral of Dmitri Boleslavovich, the head of the Shostakovich family, in the Alexander Nevsky Monastery," wrote Elena Trusova, a Petrograd musicologist. "Friends went up to poor Maria and Mrs. Shostakovich by the fresh grave to offer their condolences. Dmitri and Zoya stood a little off to one side on a mound of newly dug earth. Zoya's distraught little face was wet with tears and her coat was unfastened. Dmitri stood, his cap crushed under his arm, slowly wiping his spectacles. His eyes looked especially defenseless without them, but his entire face was filled with inward con-

centration and composure. No need to go to him with condolences!"

After the first days of mourning, which passed as if in a
haze, the family had to confront the pressing issue of earning
a livelihood. Dmitri was fifteen. He considered himself an
adult and, being the only man left in the family, held the then
traditional view that he was its natural head and had to
take care of the others; therefore, he must give up his studies
and look urgently for a job. He told his mother of his decision but ran up against her unflinching opposition. To allow
him to take such a step would ruin his future; she was fully
aware of the promise that future held, given her son's enormous talent, and could not reconcile herself to its loss. Forbidding him to change his current way of living in any way,
she herself went out to work, at first as a mere cashier. Her
qualifications as a pianist and teacher had lost their value
after many years without practice, and her children had
gone from her to Glyasser for lessons.

After a few months she received an offer to work as a
typist in the office of the Central Department of Weights and
Measures, where her husband was still remembered; in his
later years he had returned to his former place of work,
though in a far more responsible position—a position now
taken over by Mrs. Shostakovich's brother, Yakov Kokoulin.
Meanwhile Maria ended her piano classes at the Conservatory with Rozanova and took private lessons. A few months
later, when she received her pianist's diploma, she went to
work at the College of Choreography. So the financial question was settled for the time being, and Dmitri could continue
his education uninterrupted.

The loss of his father left a painful wound in Dmitri's
heart. To express the anguish, pain, and bitterness of his loss,
the young composer turned to music and produced the most

important composition of his Conservatory years: a Suite for Two Pianos dedicated to the memory of his father. The four movements—*Prelude, Fantastic Dance, Nocturne,* and *Finale* —are in varying moods. They paint a picture of deep thought and life going on all around, and bright lyricism and manly, restrained grief. The suite clearly reveals Shostakovich's enormous gift for melody, his superlative sense of form, and the tragic bent of much of his later work. The choice of genre—a composition for two performers, two pianists—was no accident: he played the piece himself with Maria. It was a joint offering from them to their late father.

The time when he would leave the piano faculty was approaching, and he was working on the program for his graduation concert. He was a brilliant pianist. His technique, especially his finger technique, was superb. Problems did not seem to exist for him. But of course the attraction of his playing did not lie in technique alone: he possessed an enormous and highly unusual talent. Under his fingers any composition, however well-known, sounded fresh and original— unexpected and even paradoxical in interpretation, but always convincing.

Whatever Dmitri played, the piano sounded as if it were not one instrument but a whole ensemble: he could pick out subtle percussive or bell-like effects he noticed in the music, producing at times almost a pizzicato, then a full tutti when required, as if he were playing a complete orchestra. The most immediately noticeable characteristic of his playing was his individualistic piano style, which had developed under the influence of his own compositions with their distinguishing features—breadth, pungency vital immediacy, the analytical power of the musical thought, and the conciseness and extreme precision with which the composer set out his ideas.

The final examination consisted of two concert performances. At the first he had to play a number of solo pieces of different styles: the Prelude and Fugue in F# Minor from the first book of J. S. Bach's *Well-Tempered Clavier*, Beethoven's Sonata no. 21, Mozart's C Major Variations, Chopin's Third Ballade, Schumann's *Humoreske*, and the piece "Venice and Naples" from Liszt's *Years of Pilgrimage*.

This complex and varied program he performed superbly; the board of examiners awarded him top marks.

The following day he played Schumann's Concerto for Piano and Orchestra with rather less success, but there was good reason for that. Early in 1923 Shostakovich had begun to be troubled by pains in the region of his neck. At first he attached no importance to them; later, when his overall condition deteriorated, he sought medical advice. The diagnosis was not reassuring: he had tuberculosis of the bronchial and lymphatic glands. At Grekov's recommendation he was sent to the clinic run by the famous Petrograd lung specialist, Professor Sternberg, where he underwent an operation, after which he was advised to go the South to convalesce.

The illness and the operation would have been reason enough to postpone his final examination, and this was proposed. He, however, adamantly refused: he still had to graduate from the composition faculty, and had to think also about getting a job and helping his mother and sister. So he began working for his examinations before he had recovered from the operation, a bandage around his throat. It is hardly surprising, then, that the tremendous nervous and physical strain proved too much for a boy who had been delicate since birth and was now weakened by serious illness.

That summer, after the examinations, Dmitri prepared to go the Crimea, where the doctors thought he would eventually recover in the healthy climate.

The family was in straitened circumstances, and the journey proved difficult to arrange. They could not get a *put-*

yovka—a travel and accommodation pass—for a sanatorium. Glazounov contrived to get hold of a pass to the medical facilities at the Gaspra Sanatorium, but Dmitri would have to arrange meals and accommodation locally. In addition, Mrs. Shostakovich was afraid to let her son go alone. She felt, not without reason, that he was timid and not equipped for the difficulties of living away from home. Maria would have to go with him to look after him.

Finding the money for the trip was a painful task. They borrowed from friends and sold the piano—a beloved old Diederichs with superb tone—although it was as necessary to them as the food in their mouths. But they still did not have enough, so Dmitri and his sister decided on a plan: they set out for the Crimea but gave concerts along the way. Consequently, they arrived there late. Kustodiev, an artist who had taken a room for them in Gaspra, was getting worried and wrote alarmed letters to Petrograd. Eventually, however, the Shostakoviches did turn up, a few days late but in good spirits; they had managed to earn some money and see a great deal.

They had a wonderful time in the Crimea. Dmitri went for treatment in the morning, then was free for the rest of the day. He traveled all over the district, going to Yalta, Gurzufe, and Simeiza. He got to Ai-Petri, a beautiful mountain with a crenellated peak like the walls of an ancient fortress, and the Bear Rock or Ayu-dag, which leans over the water like a bear slaking its thirst. He came to know the Crimea, hot and intoxicating, filled with the scents of wild, unfamiliar flowers, the fragrance of juniper, the smell of the sea, and the coolness of the breeze.

Not all his days were idle. There too he earned money by giving concerts. Maria wrote to their mother: "Today Dmitri plays in Alupka; he'll get a billion and he wants to spend it." Money then was not counted in rubles or even hundreds of rubles; inflation was rampant and millions changed hands like kopecks. With the billion that Dmitri earned they could live for a week at best.

Dmitri played a good deal. In the summer many musicians gathered in the Crimea, particularly from Moscow. The pianists Igumnov and Semyonov were there, and Minaev, the baritone from the Bolshoi Theater. Dmitri was the youngest, being not even seventeen, but the Muscovites had heard of him and, by all accounts, treated their young colleague with great respect. He was often asked to play and did so tirelessly, performing Schumann, Chopin, Liszt, and his own compositions.

Nevertheless, perhaps for the first time since early childhood, his thoughts were not entirely taken up with music. In the sanatorium where he went for treatment, he had met a girl. Tanya Glivenko, the daughter of a well-known Moscow literary scholar, had gone to Gaspra with her sister for a holiday at the end of the academic year. She was still in school and of the same age as Dmitri; he was seventeen on September 25, she two weeks later.

Tanya—small, slim, with thick dark hair and a round pretty face—was jolly, sociable, and extremely popular. She was always surrounded by a lively crowd, including a number of interesting and intelligent young people. The Shostakoviches joined this circle. They spent the days together swimming, playing volleyball, and walking in the neighborhood. In the evenings their new friends would come along in a group to hear the Shostakoviches perform.

Dmitri, like the other boys, could not remain indifferent to Tanya's charms. He dared not hope that she would reciprocate his feelings. Painfully shy, he was always retiring in company and afraid of attracting attention. Amid these confident, patronizing young people he felt like an ugly duckling with his bandaged neck and big round spectacles. Yet after a few days a miracle occurred—he realized that his feelings were eliciting a response. Tanya treated him with attention and kindness, and her face lit up with joy whenever they met.

Decades later when Dmitri Shostakovich, the world-famous composer, died, Tatyana Glivenko explained: "How could anybody not have loved him? Everybody did. He was so pure and open and always thought about other people—how to make things better and easier and nicer for them. He never thought or worried about himself. If there are saints on this earth, he was one. He was like that when he was young, when we met, and he remained like that to the end of his life."

Neither Maria nor Kustodiev, who was looking after them, took the youthful "seaside romance" seriously. They thought of the pair of them as children. But Tanya long remained in Shostakovich's heart.

They lived in different cities. Of course they wrote to each other. He dashed off to Moscow to see Tanya; she visited Petrograd. Mrs. Shostakovich received her brightly and was as welcoming and hospitable as ever. But Dmitri sensed that, inside, his mother resented the girl who might deprive her of her son.

After his father's death he was the family's sole pride, joy, and hope. His mother and two sisters loved him fiercely, kept jealous track of his achievements, and were simply that—jealous. Tanya was gentle and indecisive, while Dmitri was not noted for his resolve and was used to the routine of home life. So the years went by. Then, in 1929, Tanya got married.

Dmitri had returned to Petrograd in August 1923. Glazounov had once again managed to obtain financial aid for his protégé, but not enough to settle the debts and hire a piano. Dmitri had to find a job. Now that he had only one course of studies left to finish, and the doctors confirmed that his health had improved and gave no cause for alarm, Mrs. Shostakovich agreed. The search began. It was the early 1920s, however, and the country was still in turmoil; thousands of people in the labor exchanges were vainly looking for work. At last he found a job as an accompanist in a movie theater. This was a success, but it did have its drawbacks.

The cinema then was still silent. Every theater had live music playing while the film was on—a piano, a group of instrumentalists, or in some places even an orchestra. The musicians had to follow what was going on on the screen, trying to make the mood of the music match what the audience saw. Declarations of love, chase scenes, idyllic family settings, and fights were suitably accompanied by tender, lyrical melodies or stormy passages. Everyone played as best they could: some improvised, others drew on appropriate pieces from their repertoires. There were even special collections of "mood" music, complete with instructions, ranging from "Presentiments of Danger" through "Pangs of Conscience" to "Dreams of the Beloved." None of this, of course, was for talented musicians, but Dmitri approached his work in a serious and creative spirit, composing whole suites around the contents of films. This did not pass unnoticed; many music lovers began to go to the theater where he worked just to hear his brilliant improvisations.

The work was hard. The hours spent daily at the piano wore him out without bringing any creative satisfaction. After a while he found a way to make sure he did not waste the hours absolutely: during the showings he began to work on concert programs. He would practice difficult passages, cunningly incorporating them into his improvisations, slowing them down or speeding them up according to the events on the screen. He achieved such virtuosity in this exercise that, while preparing a trio dedicated to Tanya Glivenko for the public, he artfully succeeded in rehearsing it with violinist Venyamin Sher and cellist Grigori Pekker as an accompaniment to the improbable escapades of the heroes on the screen.

He wrote the trio in the early fall, drawing on memories of the Crimea. But he could compose nothing else: constant fatigue was taking its toll. Later he wrote: "Most musicians working in the cinema consider it a mire which will swallow musicians up, stifle their talent, turn them into inspired machines, and leave a deep and indelible mark."

All the next year, with short breaks, he worked in movie houses. He could not compose; a symphony he had conceived early in 1923 made hardly any progress. Meanwhile he was almost due to leave the Conservatory. In the spring of 1925 he decided to give up the work, which had grown hateful to him, and in June the symphony was finished. The young composer submitted it at the end of his composition course.

In April 1926, at the same time that he was recommended for the newly established higher degree course, it was decided to perform the symphony in public. The nineteen-year-old boy went in trepidation to see the venerable musician Nikolai Malko, principal conductor of the Leningrad Philharmonic. Malko received him kindly; he had already heard of Dmitri and his music.

Rehearsals began in early May, about ten days before the concert. For the first time Dmitri really heard as orchestral sound what he had previously imagined only in his inner ear. He was delighted: his ideas had been exactly right, and everything sounded just as he intended. He sat through all the rehearsals, wincing at every slip and inaccuracy by the performers and mentally playing along with each part. During the breaks he ran off to telephone his mother at work to tell her how things were going.

On May 12, 1926, the whole family went to the Philharmonic Hall—Mrs. Shostakovich outwardly reserved but on her mettle, ready to stand by her son come what may; quiet, smiling Maria, already convinced that everything would go well; and Zoya—the tomboy, as they thought of her—who was mischievous and wry and took nothing seriously, but was still anxious for her brother.

The concert seemed to take a painfully long time to begin. The crystal chandeliers twinkled, the musicians sauntered to their places, and the audience gathered very slowly in the hall. But then the rows of red velvet seats were filled, the hall fell silent, the orchestra froze on the stage. Malko stepped onto the platform and raised his baton.

Afterward came the applause, loud and slow to die away. He went out to take a bow—awkward, agonizingly conscious of his extremely youthful appearance, his velvet jacket, his round spectacles with thin metal frames, and the unruly tuft of hair which always poked up no matter what he did with it.

So fame came to him. Critics wrote about the symphony at length. They were amazed at the early maturity of such a young composer, and commented on his assurance and skill, predicting a great future. The First Symphony was soon heard abroad in Europe and America, under such eminent conductors as Toscanini, Stokowski, and Walter.

Of course there were critical voices as well as rapture and praise. To these Dmitri listened with particular attention. He learned. Most of all he remembered the comments of Nikolai Miaskovsky, an authoritative composer of many symphonic works, whose words impressed him by their accuracy and substance. But while he noted all that was said about his music, he did not rewrite anything. He himself could see the piece's defects: it showed the influence of many composers in whom he was interested at the time—composers who had left their mark on his harmonic language, the melodies, and some features of the orchestration. This was only natural: no artist is without his precursors, or works in a vacuum. It is not surprising that at the age of eighteen and nineteen Dmitri had not arrived at the completely personal and deeply individual style which distinguishes his mature works. But the symphony had the most important ingredient: an independent and mature underlying idea which was at once contemporary and profound—so profound that, over the decades, it has constantly revealed new facets.

In 1926 the audience, struck by the composer's youth, took the symphony to be a bright, vivacious, "spring-like" work. Some years later it was found that the lightness and freedom were mingled with sombre emotions and dramatic poignancy. Thirty years after the première some critics even began to argue that the dark, tragic, "fateful" side predominated. And only another ten or fifteen years after that did it become apparent how much freshness, youthful mischief, and wit was present alongside the tragic, the ironical, and the grotesque.

The young composer listened to all opinions on the symphony and recognized the justice of many of them, but decided to take them into account only in future works. All his life it was his invariable rule that what he had composed would not be reworked. Much later, he said he was appalled to think how much of his colleagues' time went into making countless revisions, and how much new music could have been written instead. The symphony remains as the nineteen-year-old wrote it.

[1926–1929]

Curiously, the success of his first major work did not give the composer any confidence in himself or his abilities. On the contrary, for some time he completely lost his facility for composing. "In about 1926 I went through a severe creative crisis and could not write a note," he recalled on the eve of his fiftieth birthday. "I accounted for it by saying that the sophistication of the Conservatory had destroyed my capacity for creative work. But that, of course, was incorrect."

Not only could he not write, but he went through what he had previously written and destroyed a large amount of it. Among other things, the opera *Tsygany* (The Gypsies) went into the flames.

Piano playing remained as an emotional outlet. He played a great deal, appeared in Leningrad at the Society of the Friends of Chamber Music, and went on tour to Slavyansk. In the summer of 1926 he performed with Malko in Kharkov, playing Tchaikovsky's First Concerto. His repertoire included many solo pieces spanning a long period from the birth of true piano composition to the late romantics, plus concertos by Chopin, Schumann, Tchaikovsky, and Prokofiev.

The press was always full of praise for the young artist's performances. Critics commented on the assurance, depth, and conviction of his interpretations, his faultless musical sense, his textural clarity, beautifully shaped phrasing, and filigree-precise technique. There was no doubt that a successful career as a virtuoso pianist lay ahead of him. Everyone was convinced of this, and the most impressive confirmation was about to appear.

At the end of 1926 a group of Soviet pianists was invited to take part in the first Chopin Competition in Warsaw. This was a great occasion: for the first time Soviet musicians were to participate on behalf of their country in a major international music contest. Those chosen to compete had to be the crème de la crème—worthy representatives of the artistic life of the young nation. Every musician waited eagerly to hear who had been selected. Then the news came: Lev Oborin, Grigori Ginsberg, and Yuri Bryushkov would be going from Moscow, and from Leningrad, Dmitri Shostakovich. There were many superb musicians in Nikolaev's class, but no one was surprised when the choice fell on Shostakovich.

The competition was tough and the program very difficult: the Polonaise in F♯ Minor was compulsory, and in addition each contestant had to play a ballade and a concerto, as well as two preludes, two mazurkas, two études, and two nocturnes chosen from a list drawn up by the jury. In December Shostakovich began to live like a recluse. Everything at home was arranged to allow him to work successfully. He gave up all his old habits: going to the theater and concerts, meeting friends, music-making sessions, reading, and evening walks. Instead, he worked on the pieces for the competition.

The results were striking. Bogdanov-Berezovsky, a composer and writer and one of Shostakovich's fellow students, later recalled: "His sharply personal, forcefully rhythmic, tonally rich, and at the same time finely descriptive style of playing became still more pronounced. His listeners were thrilled by the feeling of proximity to a live creative process and a sense of the originality of his musical ideas."

Nikolaev heard his pupil and was content. He was convinced that Shostakovich would emerge the winner, but things turned out differently. Before he left for Moscow, the boy suffered a severe attack of appendicitis. Everybody thought he should have an operation immediately, but he refused: come what may, he wanted to be at the competition. They went to Ivan Grekov, an old friend of the family and one of the best doctors in the city. With a heavy heart, he gave Shostakovich permission to go.

Before leaving for Warsaw, the pianists selected to compete gave a concert in Moscow, in the Great Hall of the Conservatory. This concert, the final test, aroused great public interest, and thoughtful reviews appeared in the press. Of Shostakovich, the critics wrote that he was an intelligent and thorough musician who grasped the structure of the works he played and could reveal it in every detail, and that the poetic side of the music was always to the fore in his playing. No one guessed what efforts it cost him to keep going.

The days in Warsaw were also difficult. The pains began again and grew steadily worse. He played well and the public greeted him with enthusiasm and endless ovations, but things were not in his favor. The political mood in Warsaw was tense. Counterrevolutionary Russian emigré circles were whipping up animosity against the Soviet state. Incident followed incident, and the Soviet ambassador was killed.

One school of thought held that only Polish pianists really understood Chopin or could interpret his music correctly, and considered these the only candidates for the top prizes. There were prizes for only three contestants. When it became obvious that two of them would unquestionably go to Soviet pianists—Lev Oborin and Grigori Ginsberg, who caused a sensation—the jury, made up entirely of Polish musicians, added another prize and a number of diplomas. The idea was certainly not to award them to the Russians.

When the results were announced and it was discovered

that Shostakovich had been awarded only a diploma, every-body thought it a glaring injustice and commiserated with him. Dmitri, however, swallowing his bitterness, was de-lighted for his friend Lev Oborin. Dmitri knew he could have played better—far better. But now his only concern was to go home. On his return he went into Grekov's clinic for the operation.

After the operation he was ready to work again. Now music was welling up inside him and demanding to be let out. At first, perhaps under the influence of his "pianistic" life of recent weeks, it took the form of piano pieces. One after another, from February 25 to April 7, 1927, appeared ten miniatures for piano: *Recitative, Serenade, Nocturne, Elegy, Étude, Funeral March, Dance of Death, Canon, Legend*, and *Cradle Song*, known collectively as the *Aphorisms*.

After living with Chopin's music for so long, Shostakovich seemed to be experimenting, altering the significance of piano forms which had become traditional. There was also an ele-ment of mischief, a desire to shock the public. It was no accident that the tune hiccuped in the *Serenade* or that the *Nocturne* growled and was submerged under stormy figura-tions. But on a serious level Shostakovich also wanted to explore the possibilities of small-scale instrumental forms and experiment with them, seeking his own style and com-municating his vision of the world.

For old times' sake, he showed the *Aphorisms* to his men-tor at the Conservatory, Professor Steinberg. But Steinberg, a strict academician who had been Rimsky-Korsakov's favorite pupil, and who was a devout guardian of the classical tradi-tion within the walls of the oldest Russian musical institu-tion, said that he could not understand such music. For him it was alien and inspired nothing except bafflement. From then on, Dmitri ceased to show Steinberg his music. The paths of teacher and pupil parted for good.

After the *Aphorisms* Dmitri began composing an entirely different work, the Second Symphony. The young composer's new symphonic work was dedicated to the tenth anniversary of the October Revolution. He had used this theme before: his First Sonata for Piano, written a year earlier, had been subtitled *October*. "In its naked passion and inexhaustible, elemental force," wrote the music critic M. Grinberg, "the sonata comes across like an explosion, a protest, like liberation and a break with the past." And now there was a symphony devoted to the same subject. Dmitri was burning with an idea which, half a century later, may seem a little naive: to write a symphonic tribute to each of the important events in the revolutionary calendar. The Second Symphony, which he called a symphonic offering "to October," was to open this cycle of commemorative works.

The symphony was a one-movement work for orchestra with a choral finale. Dmitri chose stirring poetry by Alexander Bezymensky in praise of struggle, the October Revolution, the Commune, and Lenin. The work was written in free form, making extensive use of imitative sound effects, and expressed many features of the age which formed part of the composer's vivid, immediate impressions. In the years following the Revolution, art for the first time had been intended for the whole population and became a vehicle for inspiring the masses. It moved out into city streets and squares, reaching literally the whole of the people. Inspired by the great deeds of the October Revolution, the artists, musicians, and actors of Petrograd took to putting on grand "events," following the example of the mass celebrations during the French Revolution. *The Capture of the Winter Palace*, dedicated to the memorable events of 1917, was staged on Petrograd's squares and embankments on November 7, 1920, with military units, brass bands, and choirs of thousands taking part; the audience generally joined in during the choral parts.

Political slogans and countless sound effects—the boom of cannon, the rattle of rifle fire, and the roar of engines—found their way into many theatrical and musical productions of the period. The same ideas were also reflected in the underlying concept of Shostakovich's Second Symphony, although the music was not in the least overtly pictorial. The symphony's structure reproduced a scheme prevalent at that time: from a chaos symbolizing the dark history of the Russian people, their subjection, and their lack of rights, it passed through protest and struggle to the victory celebrated in the closing part of the work.

The symphony was performed during the public holidays of November 1927 and met a favorable reception. "The idea of the revolution in the *October* Symphony is conveyed in the forceful, huge-scale, dynamically explosive deployment of the composer's vital creative powers," one critic commented. Thus began a spell of intense creativity and enormous artistic achievements.

Shostakovich's acquaintance, or rather the beginning of his highly auspicious friendship, with Ivan Sollertinsky dates from this period. The very beginning—what might be called the prehistory of their friendship—dates back to 1919, when the young Conservatory student began to attend Philharmonic concerts regularly. Young music lovers generally got standing-room tickets, which were cheaper. In the intermission they would fetch coats from the cloakroom or produce newspapers, spread them on the floor in the gallery, and make themselves comfortable. Among the regular concertgoers, Dmitri soon became aware of a fairly tall, stooping, thick-lipped young man with piercingly intelligent eyes. This man seemed to experience enormous pleasure as he listened to the music, and afterward invariably discussed his impressions with his friends interestingly and at length. His name was Sollertinsky, and he was a legend in Petrograd.

Years later Shostakovich spoke of his friend and his untimely death:

Mutual friends told me that he knew every language that was or ever had been spoken on earth, and that he knew about all kinds of sciences, and that he knew the whole of Shakespeare, Pushkin, Gogol, Aristotle, and Plato by heart, and that he knew—in short, everything. I gained the impression right away that he was someone out of the ordinary and difficult and awkward for an average person to get along with; in 1921, when a friend introduced me to Sollertinsky, I backed off as quickly as I could, feeling it would be too difficult to carry on an acquaintance with such an unusual man.

Our next meeting was in 1926. The Leningrad students were taking an exam in Marxism-Leninism so as to be able to go on for a higher degree. Among the people waiting to be called before the board of examiners was Sollertinsky. Before the exam I was nervous. Presently, Sollertinsky was called in. Very soon he came out again. I plucked up courage and asked him: "Excuse me, was the exam very difficult?" "No, not at all," he replied. "What did they ask you?" "Oh, the easiest things: the growth of materialism in Ancient Greece; Sophocles' poetry as an expression of materialist tendencies; English seventeenth-century philosophers and something else besides!"

Need I say that I was filled with horror at his reply? Finally, in 1927, I met him at the home of a Leningrad musician. There weren't many guests, just three or four including Sollertinsky and myself. The time passed quickly, without our noticing. I was completely bowled over when Sollertinsky turned out to be an uncommonly merry, simple, brilliantly witty, and entirely down-to-earth person. Our excellent host kept us until late, then Sollertinsky and I walked home. We lived in the same neighborhood. The way seemed short because walking with him was no effort: he spoke so interestingly about the most varied aspects of life and art. During the conversation it emerged that I didn't know a single foreign language, while he couldn't play the piano. So the very next day Sollertinsky gave me my first lesson in German and I gave him a lesson on the piano. The lessons came to a swift and unsuccessful end: I didn't learn German and Sollertinsky didn't learn to play the piano, but we still remained great friends to the very end of his remarkable life.

From that evening on they were literally inseparable, seeing each other daily. Normally Sollertinsky would drop by the Shostakoviches', the two of them would settle down in one of the rooms, and the others in the house would hear music, animated voices, and frequent bursts of laughter. If they could not meet, they would talk several times a day on the telephone. If even that failed, they would run over to each other's house (fortunately, they lived in the same neighborhood) and leave notes. They complemented each other remarkably well: Sollertinsky incomparably erudite, a brilliant polemicist and orator, witty, caustic, never at a loss; and the shy, painfully impressionable Shostakovich, who nonetheless had his own acute vision of the world.

Their influence on each other was enormous. Until 1927, at all events, Sollertinsky's professional interests, for all his love of music, were inclined more toward literature and drama. A philologist and Spanish scholar by training, he had written about Spanish literature, Lope de Vega, Molière's comedies, and Shakespeare's *Hamlet*. Everything he had published up to 1927 concerned the theater or ballet, of which he was also a great admirer. It is indicative that his first review of an opera—Křenek's *Johnny*—was written in November 1928, after he became friends with Shostakovich.

Sollertinsky's activities then shifted for good into the musical field. He later became artistic director of the Leningrad Philharmonic, a professor at the Conservatory, and the author of many works on musicology.

The influence in the other direction was no less strong. On the eve of his fiftieth birthday, Shostakovich recalled: "I got a great deal out of my friendship with Sollertinsky, who was a highly gifted man and a talented musicologist with a truly encyclopedic knowledge and a broad, artistic outlook. People have tried to accuse him of being a bad influence on me, but in fact he was always trying to extend my outlook. Sollertinsky imbued me with an interest in music 'from Bach to Offenbach,' so to speak."

Of course the influence was not just musical. Sollertinsky shared the whole wealth of his learning in the field of literature, philosophy, art history and history in general, and the theater and ballet with his younger friend. But this was not the chief factor in their relationship. They were mutually indispensable to the extent that, if parted for a few days, they pined hopelessly and wrote long, detailed letters describing everything that had happened, sometimes inventing things, fantasizing, each sure that he would be correctly understood. Their letters touched on both business and artistic questions and on matters affecting their private lives. Almost always a note of sadness at being away from each other crept in. Yet their periods apart were generally very short. The first occurred almost immediately, in 1927.

That summer Shostakovich went to stay in the small town of Detskoye Selo outside Leningrad, where he lived in the *Dom Uchonykh* (Scholars' Resort); in the evening he walked in the splendid park and played tennis, while during the day, being unused to idleness, he thought over his newest ideas. On August 20 he sent from there the first of the letters preserved in Sollertinsky's archives:

Exceptionally pleased to receive a postcard from you. You squeeze so many important ideas and insights into so small a space, one can only marvel. I haven't written before because I was in a bad mood, for Muzsektor [Music Department of the Ministry of Culture] only yesterday sent me the 500 rubles. As a result, my mood improved and I decided to write you. Tomorrow I go to Moscow. Muzsektor sent me a telegram telling me to go for a demonstration of my revolutionary music. *The Nose* is coming along. So is my German. My next letter, probably on Wednesday, will close with the words *mein lieber Iwan Iwanowitsch*.

Yours,
D. Shostakovich

Shostakovich's financial position continued to be very difficult: he had no job and was living on his graduate student grant. Since the royalties for the *October* Symphony were an extremely important supplement to his budget, no wonder the delay in getting paid adversely affected his spirits. As for his German, it remained at about the level demonstrated at the end of the letter. What is most significant in the letter, however, is the reference to *The Nose*, an opera the outline of which was exercising his mind greatly.

Gogol was one of Shostakovich's favorite authors. This highly original writer, whose works were always so remarkable in combining realism with fantasy, the humdrum with the grotesque, a love of Russia with a hatred of the autocratic regime's "leaden abominations," had fascinated the composer from his earliest childhood. Even before he went to the Conservatory, one of his first inspirations had been an opera based on Gogol called *The Dreadful Revenge*. Shostakovich did not just like Gogol; he was very close to him in temperament.

For his first opera the young Shostakovich selected a remarkable subject. He was fascinated by a brilliant piece of

Gogolian grotesque: the tale of how a nose runs away from a middle-ranking government official named Kovalyov, a college inspector, and drives around St. Petersburg wearing the uniform of one of the highest civil service grades in Tsarist Russia. *The Nose* interested Shostakovich because of its sharp contrast of realism with fantasy, its biting irony and withering sarcasm. Later, in an article entitled "Before the première" published in *Rabochii i teatr* (The Worker and the Theater) in 1930, the composer wrote: "Nowadays an opera on a classical subject will be more relevant if the subject is satirical." But the attraction was not just the satirical element. As Shostakovich admitted much later, he simply "wanted to have some fun." Indeed, mischief and infectious gaiety spring from the pages of this youthful yet completely mature masterpiece.

Shostakovich decided to outline the libretto himself. Gogol's text turned out to contain too little material, but the composer was not prepared to write his own, so where he needed words that were not in the story he borrowed from other works. As a result, phrases from *May Nights, Taras Bulba, Landowners of the Old School,* and *A Tale of How Ivan Ivanovich Quarreled with Ivan Nikiforovich* appear in the libretto. The only part of the opera not by Gogol is the aria by Ivan, Kovalyov's servant, in Scene 6, which is Smerdyakov's romance from Dostoevsky's *Brothers Karamazov*.

Naturally, Shostakovich did not feel he could take upon himself so weighty a task as writing a full operatic libretto. Having decided exactly what he needed, he went in search of assistance. The writers Yonin, Preis, and Zamyatin offered to help. So as to present Gogol's story as fully as possible, the authors constructed the libretto on much the same lines as a film script, with many scene changes and sequences. This obviously reflected both Shostakovich's considerable experience in the cinema and the powerful impression made on him recently by Alban Berg's operatic masterpiece *Wozzeck*, which was performed in Leningrad in 1926.

In addition, Shostakovich was interested in drama and would soon begin writing music for theatrical productions. But even before that the young musician was intrigued by some interesting theatrical experiments. And of course he could not miss his favorite author: in the spring of 1927 a new production of Gogol's *Government Inspector* opened in a Leningrad theater. Those who saw the production, by Igor Terentiev, remember it as a theatrical landmark. That this cutting, bizarre play, with its pathos of discovering the lunacy of the world around us, created an enormous impression on Shostakovich, is borne out by the resemblances noted by researchers between *The Government Inspector* in Terentiev's production and the final version of the libretto for *The Nose*.

Shostakovich loved Gogol's story and delightful dialogue, and tried to render them as fully and accurately as possible. He was most concerned to have a clear, graphic presentation of the text and stressed that the music should not be an end in itself. He avoided old, accepted operatic forms and wrote vocal parts in a declamatory, recitative style.

Obviously, this treatment of an opera was not Shostakovich's own invention. There were precedents in Russian music, the first being Dargomyzhsky's chamber opera *The Stone Guest*, set to the complete and entirely unaltered text of one of Pushkin's brilliant minor tragedies, which was almost all in the form of recitatives. Another precedent, still closer in time to Shostakovich, was Moussorgsky's comic opera *The Wedding*, also based on a work by Gogol. Shostakovich used these examples as a point of departure for his own first opera. Other influences were also at work, as mentioned earlier.

The opera was composed in spurts: Shostakovich began it in the summer of 1927, then broke off work for some time, then composed the second act in Moscow in January 1928.

Shostakovich's temporary move to Moscow was connected with an important event in his life: Meyerhold, the famous producer who was then at the height of his fame, had invited him to head the musical department at his theater, and Shostakovich of course accepted. Money was still a problem for him; he lived mainly on his student grant. Sometimes he received royalties for a composition or a concert appearance, but this income was unreliable. Now at last, however, he had the prospect of a quiet life and a secure income, part of which he could send to his mother and Maria.

He felt an obligation toward his elder sister. After his father's death she and his mother had supported both Zoya and himself even though he, almost an adult, should have shouldered the responsibility for the family's welfare. Had it not been for his mother's unbending determination, he would of course have done so, but it is not certain whether any good would have come of it. He would probably have become ill sooner and been unable to finish at the Conservatory.

Shostakovich settled down comfortably in Moscow. Meyerhold showed the utmost concern for him, put him up in his apartment, and treated him like a father. Duties at the theater were not onerous. Meyerhold liked to rehearse to music, so Shostakovich compiled various musical extracts for this purpose. He also maintained the correspondence with composers commissioned to write incidental music for various productions. When a piece of music was called for during a play, he went out on stage and played the piano. In a certain sense he became an actor: in *The Government Inspector* he went on stage in a frock coat, trying to behave naturally, sat down at the piano, and accompanied an actress singing a romance by Glinka. But he preferred to be in the orchestra pit, away from the eyes of the audience, where no one paid any attention to him.

It was during his time free from these simple duties that Shostakovich wrote the second act of *The Nose*. He worked intensively on the opera during the day, then devoted his evenings to interesting people. He met Kerzhentsevy, who had been ambassador in Rome and later chairman of the Arts Committee; Sergei Eisenstein, the film producer who made the famous film *Battleship Potemkin*; and Lunacharsky. Thus the People's Commissar for Education finally met the musician whom he had heard of so long ago from Gorky and Glazounov.

Shostakovich was truly captivated by the theater. In his next letter to Sollertinsky, he wrote:

> I go to the theater whenever I can. Apart from all Meyerhold's productions, I've seen *The Armored Train** and *Days of the Turbins*† at the Arts,‡ *The Breakup*§ at the Vakhtangov studio, and much more.
>
> As a play, *The Armored Train* works particularly well. *Days of the Turbins* has some truly tragic moments, and people were sobbing loudly in the theater. But it was all spoiled by the last act and the official ending. The play which impresses me most is still *The Government Inspector* at Meyerhold's theater. I have now seen it through about three times. Seven times in all. And the more I see it, the more I like it.

Things, it seems, could not have been better. But as time passed, living away from Leningrad became increasingly difficult. Shostakovich loved his mother and sisters dearly and missed them. He also missed his new friend Sollertinsky,

---

* *Armored Train 14–69*, by Ivanov.
† By Bulgakov.
‡ Moscow Academy Theater of the Arts.
§ By Lavrenev.

although from his first days there he poured out his soul to him in long, detailed letters humorously describing every facet of Moscow life. Moreover, he was getting tired of always arranging other people's music and, most of all, of having to abandon his ideas and accept the producer's instead. In the spring of 1928 he finally left Moscow.

His departure did not at all signal a break with Meyerhold. That fall, when Meyerhold's theater was given Mayakovsky's play *The Bedbug* to stage, Shostakovich was commissioned to write the music. He composed it in Leningrad, sending movements to Meyerhold as he finished them, and when the job was done he went to present the full score in the theater, in the presence of the author and the actors.

On that occasion a curious incident took place which demonstrated that, for all his modesty and shyness, Shostakovich could stand up for himself and defend his dignity. When introduced to him, Mayakovsky—tall, noisy, and self-confident—looked down condescendingly on this young composer who seemed no more than a boy, and grandly held out two fingers for him to shake. In response, Shostakovich also held out two fingers. Meyerhold, embarrassed, tried to ease the situation by explaining to the composer that Mayakovsky had developed pains in his hand. To this, Shostakovich replied in his usual brief way, "But I've just developed pains in my hand, too!"

This minor episode had no effect on relations within the group: work on *The Bedbug* went ahead in an atmosphere of complete cordiality. But all this was much later, after *The Nose* had been put on at the Leningrad Maly Opera. Shostakovich had completed the work in the spring of 1928, on his return to Leningrad. It proved to be bright, colorful, inventive, and rhythmically rich, testifying to the composer's uncommon talent and keen sense of humor. "Despite all the comedy on stage, the music is not comic," Shostakovich stressed. "I think this is correct, since Gogol describes all his comic events in serious language. That is the strength and value of Gogol's humor. He is not 'flip.' The music also tries not to be 'flip.'"

It was not. It was simply witty, abundantly resourceful, infectiously gay, and at times sarcastic and stinging. The audience, after all, was watching a satire on the Russia of Tsar Nicolas I, murderer of the Decembrists and oppressor of freedom, not just a light anecdote from the life of the St. Petersburg gentry!

The opera was finished at the beginning of May. Sollertinsky was an enthusiastic supporter of the new work. He took the composer to the Leningrad Maly Opera and interested the principal conductor, Samuel Samosud, and the producer Smolich in staging the opera. It was accepted. On July 20, having gone to his friend's house and found him out, Shostakovich left a note on a calling card: "Dear Ivan Ivanovich, I just got a call from the *Vechernyaya Krasnaya Gazeta* [Red Evening Gazette] asking me to write about *The Nose* for their 'Coming Next Season' column. I'd be extremely grateful if you could find the time to come over *today*, since I must hand the article in tomorrow and would like you to read what I've written. D. Shostakovich."

On July 24 the paper carried an interview with Shostakovich. About his opera, he said:

> I did not feel it necessary to strengthen Gogol's satirical text by music with an "ironic" or "parodic" flavor; instead, I gave it a totally serious musical accompaniment. The contrast between the comic action and the serious, symphonic-style music is used to create the basic theatrical effect; this seems the more justified in that Gogol himself describes the comic wanderings of his subject in deliberately serious language. . . .
>
> The music is an unbroken symphonic texture, not a se-

quence of "numbers," but without any system of leitmotifs. Each act forms part of a single musical and dramatic symphony. The chorus and vocal ensembles play an important part.

But the première of *The Nose* did not take place the following season, for the play was still not ready. Shostakovich, impatient to hear as soon as possible how at least parts of it really sounded, put together a suite consisting of the overture, Kovalyov's aria, the two entr'actes, Ivan's song, Kovalyov's monologue, and the galop representing Kovalyov riding in the carriage. He gave the score to Nikolai Malko, who conducted it in Moscow. Reviews of the concert were encouraging; the music aroused interest in this artistic experiment in the tradition established by Moussorgsky.

The première of the opera was set for 1929. A preview of extracts was arranged beforehand and a concert performance was given on June 16. Then the debate began and it was not merely stormy, it was savage. Some of the musicians, members of the RAPM (Russian Association of Proletarian Musicians), accused the composer of every sin known to mortal man: writing music which the ordinary listener could not understand, ignoring contemporary reality, deliberately escaping from Soviet themes into anecdote. Shostakovich was condemned for formalism and empty display.

Despite such serious allegations, work on the opera was allowed to continue. Every fragment, every bar, every scene was worked on with special care. Shortly before the première, extracts were performed for Leningrad factory workers in one of the city's Houses of Culture. The unsophisticated audience, lacking established musical tastes and habits and unaware of traditional views on opera, trustingly accepted the composer's ideas and judged the work according to its true worth.

[1929–1930]

The end of the 1920s and the beginning of the 1930s form a remarkable period in Shostakovich's life because of the intensity with which he worked, the range of genres covered, and the scale of his projects. It was the first flowering of genius, when countless ideas occur one after another, sometimes simultaneously, and a musician is attracted by many different subjects and is full of things he wants to say.

Unexpectedly, at the end of 1928, Shostakovich returned to film music—in another capacity, of course, since he had sworn never to go back to being a movie-house pianist. With every month that passed, film makers were growing less satisfied with the standard of musical accompaniment to their films, and in Leningrad they decided to do something about it. The board of the Sovkino studio in Leningrad sent a letter to Moscow:

> It would seem more natural and logical for the producer to agree with a composer while making the film, and in particular for them to agree finally on the musical scenario when the picture is being put together. . . . This method . . . in most cases will give us a genuinely artistic and sometimes even talented musical work, especially if one considers that there are in Leningrad a good many important young musical figures. . . . It should be mentioned that the producers of *New Babylon* are currently looking for a suitable composer to write the musical scenario.

The producers Kozintsev and Trauberg found a "suitable composer"—Shostakovich. Having seen the still unassembled reels of film about an assistant in the Paris store *New Babylon* and her soldier sweetheart, who find themselves in opposing camps during the Paris Commune, Shostakovich agreed to write the music. Kozintsev later recalled: "We had the same idea: not to illustrate shots, but to give them a new quality and scope; the music had to be composed against the external events so as to show the inner sense of the action. . . . In many respects it foreshadowed talkies: the character of the screen changed."

Shostakovich gladly got down to work. The music, abounding in happy inventions, was ready in a very short time. In addition to his own themes, Shostakovich used extracts from Offenbach's popular operettas, a subtle orchestration of the *Old French Song* from Tchaikovsky's *Children's Album*, and a heroic setting of the Marseillaise. The score was for a modest instrumental group but was nevertheless filled with different sonorities, masterly part-writing, and brash theatrical effects. But it met with a sad fate: the cinema orchestra leaders had no desire to waste time learning difficult and unconventional music, especially since they were also losing the pay they normally received for compiling and arranging film accompaniments. Having heard the score at a preview, they decided to block it. Their views were expressed by the conductor at the *Piccadilly*, one Vladimirov. Kozintsev remembers a conversation during which Vladimirov stated: "It's not enough that the man doesn't understand the cinema —he's cocksure as well! I offered to help him orchestrate his music and he refused."

In this tense, nervous climate Shostakovich wrote a unique letter, a cry for help:

Dear Ivan Ivanovich,

I have a great favor to ask. Come to the *Piccadilly* tonight at 8. I'm inviting you and the artistic staff from the film studio personally. They have given us two boxes. After the film there will be a discussion of my music. Can I ask you, unofficially, to do what you can to rehabilitate me if they hurl abuse? If Vladimirov says my music can't be played by a trio or some other group, you say it can. Say they must use the piano reduction and the orchestral parts they need for that ensemble.

If you can, phone me before you leave for the *Piccadilly*.

D. Shostakovich. 22.iii.1929

In spite of all his efforts, the music could not be saved. The conductors had agreed on their verdict and denounced the music and its composer roundly, refused to learn the piece, and played it so badly that the producers were forced to take it off the second day the film was shown. This brilliant work by the youthful Shostakovich lay in the archives for half a century before it found performers and an audience.*

Finally, in the summer of 1929, Shostakovich went south for a holiday. He planned to go by train from Leningrad to Sebastopol and from there by boat to Sukhumi on the Caucasian coast. He also intended to visit other towns in the Caucasus. At the end of May he left for Sebastopol, where he spent two days looking around the city and visiting the excavations of ancient Khersones, then on July 5 sailed for Sukhumi. From Sukhumi he traveled along the coast to a small place called Gudauta, where he resolved to spend a month.

When he arrived, the composer was thinking only of taking a rest. The winter had been busy and difficult, and the recent journey—despite its interest, or maybe because of it—

* A suite of music from the film has been recorded by a group of soloists from the Moscow Philharmonic under Gennadi Rozhdestvensky. Rozhdestvensky reconstructed the score from the extant orchestral parts and compiled the suite.

had been exhausting. But after only ten days his mood was changing. "I'm living well. I work a lot, but even so, I'm relaxing," he wrote. He was working on his Third Symphony.

The symphony, entitled the *First of May*, had been conceived as the next part of the cycle dedicated to the Red Revolution. Like its predecessor, the Second, it was in one movement and had a choral finale. From Gudauta he wrote to the conductor Alexander Gauk, asking him to conduct this "freshly baked symphony."

Meanwhile he intended to complete his successful holiday. "I leave here on the 28th. First stop, Batum, by boat. Then by train to Tiflis. From Tiflis along the Georgian military road to Vladikavkaz.* From there to Pyatigorsk, and then by plane to Moscow. Please keep quiet about the airplane. If word gets to mother she'll go out of her mind with fright. From Moscow to Leningrad probably on foot, for I'm afraid the money won't last. It should, but I'm incapable of budgeting."

Reading these lines, one is reminded of something often obscured by the quantity and maturity of the music: the composer was very young. He drank in impressions like a teen-ager, trying to see as much as possible and visit every place he could.

The 1929–1930 season proved very busy. Rehearsals for *The Nose* were in progress and he took an extremely active interest in them. The Philharmonic was preparing for the première of the *First of May* Symphony, which also occupied his thoughts and time. When Meyerhold approached him about writing the music for Mayakovsky's comedy *The Bedbug*, Shostakovich took up the proposal enthusiastically. Al-

* Now Ordzhonikidze.

most simultaneously he was writing music for other theater productions in Leningrad: Bezymensky's play *The Shot*, and Gorbenko and Lvov's *Virgin Soil*. Beyond that, he had begun work on a composition in what was for him a new genre—his first ballet.

Shostakovich had been drawn to ballet since his Conservatory days. A fellow student in the composition faculty, Bogdanov-Berezovsky, with whom Shostakovich was for a time quite close, recalled how, after a full day at the Conservatory, they would run across the square to the theater to watch *Sleeping Beauty* or *La fille mal gardée* for the umpteenth time.

The art of ballet was at a very difficult stage. While, on the whole, classical opera had been retained as a model for Soviet musicians, who sought to follow (or occasionally to revive) the traditions of Glinka, Tchaikovsky, Dargomyzhsky, Moussorgsky, and Borodin, the situation in ballet was entirely different. In contrast with opera, which dealt with large themes and often carried messages concerning liberation, social protest, or patriotism, ballet was primarily for entertainment. Developing in the courts of the French kings, it had remained a court entertainment for centuries, and was still regarded as such at the end of the 1920s, despite the outstanding Russian ballet and its world-wide reputation linked with the names of Tchaikovsky and Glazounov, Petipa and Fokine, and Diaghilev's renowned company.

With few exceptions, the themes of ballets were fairy tales or legends; there was nothing topical in them. Those involved in the growing field of Soviet ballet could not be satisfied with such a situation and began to look for new approaches. There were many experiments, some of them failures, but they persevered, looking for new subjects and a new choreographic language.

In 1929 the Directorate of Theaters held a competition for the best ballet scenario drawn from contemporary life. The winning entry was *Dinamiada*, by Ivanovsky, the film producer. The action of the ballet (in its final version it was entitled *The Golden Age*) takes place in a large city outside Russia, where a Soviet soccer team has arrived for a world tournament. There they run into fascists who wish to provoke the Soviet athletes. The captain of the Soviet team is attacked by drunken youths and later, when the Soviet players win their match, the captain and several players are arrested. They are then freed by workers. The heroes are characterized in scenes depicting sports events—the movements of fencers, tennis players, and boxers translated into dance, with grand processions and exuberant folk dancing. These are contrasted with caricatured dance styles—foxtrots, tangos, cancans, and tap dances. The ballet ends with a dance of proletarian solidarity.

The libretto was offered to Shostakovich, who decided to try his hand at the new genre. During the summer and fall of 1929, he wrote thirty-seven numbers in different styles—acrobatic dances for the athletes, and pantomimes and satirical episodes. "Theater music should not 'accompany,'" he wrote in the booklet prepared for the presentation of the ballet on stage. "It should have a positive influence. Failure to obey this rule relegates the music to the background, despite the fact that it has enormous capacity for influencing people. I felt it was essential not just to write music that people could dance to, but to dramatize the musical aspect and give the score real symphonic tension and dramatic movement."

The notions on which the composer based his work were absolutely correct, but were applied to a libretto written according to the rules of the stage and clearly conceived for it. As ballet historians today correctly observe, "The music generated symphonic tension and dramatic movement of a level to which the play did not rise."

This conclusion was drawn later, at the première in the autumn of 1930. Meanwhile, having handed in the score to the old Mariinsky Theater, Shostakovich could devote more time to his other favorite activity—concert performance. In early February 1930 he went to Rostov-on-Don, where he played Tchaikovsky's First Concerto; his symphony was performed at the same time. He was invited by the musicians of Rostov to give a lecture on the current status of music. On spare evenings he went to the Rostov theater, which was first-class, and to concerts. The weather, however, was oppressive and could change surprisingly fast: when he arrived it was very warm, but suddenly there came a 27-degree frost and a terrible wind, bringing clouds of dust from the steppes. In the brief lulls, Shostakovich walked around and got to know the city.

As always he wrote long, detailed letters to his friend: "I had a telegram from mother saying that *The Nose* was sold out on the 8th. I'm pleased, but I fear it isn't true and Mother just wants to cheer me up. I don't know when I'll be back. Most of all I regret missing performances of *The Nose*, but maybe it will still run for a performance or so after I get back."

He had time to see *The Nose*. It played fourteen times from its première to the end of the season—almost a record. But the following season it disappeared from the repertoire. Drawing the depressing conclusion, the prominent musical figure B. Asafyev, later a member of the Academy of Sciences, wrote: "The fate of that talented opera *The Nose* is sad indeed. When the young composer had the courage to use music to open up true Gogolian life and hence do away with the figures from the past which troubled his imagination, he was subjected to rude criticism instead of careful appraisal."

In the summer of 1930 Shostakovich again decided to travel. This time, in addition to Tiflis, which he had already seen, he chose to visit Baku, the capital of Azerbaijan, and then the wonderful town of Odessa on the coast. Under the influence of his film-making friends, he changed his plans and began his trip from Odessa, where he arrived on July 17. He liked the city enormously. "I shall spend a long time here," he wrote in his next letter. "I'm living very well, which means I'm working a lot. What, after all, can be grander for an artist than constant, uninterrupted activity?"

He was now at work on his second ballet, *Bolt*. The plot was rather stupid and naive, yet he had accepted the commission. Why? Probably his youth was the cause: it was silly, but he wanted to write music, to compose prolifically in all genres. It was a challenge to overcome the bad libretto with his music and prove he could do anything with it. The libretto was later redone, but even in its revised form it did not differ greatly from the original. The ballet naturally came in for a lot of criticism, but the music worked. It was happy and playful, and one could really dance to it.

Just as he had done when writing his first ballet, Shostakovich made use of the experience he had gained in his work with the Young Workers Theater—TRAM—a lively theater where young workers took part in artless plays depicting the realities of factory life. The music for these plays was rigorous and inventive—songs, marches, dances, tableaux. That is also how Shostakovich wrote his ballets *The Golden Age* and *Bolt*, paying little heed to the dramatic element in the music for the production. He took the same approach in his last ballet, written some years later—*The Glittering Stream*.

At the same time as *Bolt*, Shostakovich was working on

his first sound film, *Girl Alone*, produced by Kozintsev and Trauberg. After a month of working in Odessa, in August he left for the Caucasus to revisit Gudauta, which he had liked so much. Then, in mid-September, he returned to Odessa to continue working on the music for the film.

The end of the year was frantic: he had to hand in the score of *Bolt* on January 1, while filming was coming to an end in Kiev and he had to be there. This time the music and the film were created together. The sound director was Lev Arnshtam, a former pianist and fellow student of Shostakovich's at the Conservatory who loved his music, and who later became a prominent Soviet film producer. "Shostakovich's music was really something!" Kozintsev said later. "And they couldn't do anything about it—either foul it up with the tinny orchestras from the *Piccadilly* or the *Parisiany*, or replace it with a mishmash from the *Cinema Music* album!"

But the composer's thoughts were already on a new work —an opera based on Leskov's novella, *Lady Macbeth of Mtsensk District*.

[1930–1934]

Almost fifteen years earlier a significant encounter had taken place in Shostakovich's life; it was with a man much older than himself, a man old enough to be his father: the artist Boris Kustodiev. Their acquaintance had begun by chance. The artist's daughter Irina was at the same school as Shostakovich, but a year ahead of him. One day she heard him at an open evening, playing the Grieg sonata and pieces by Chopin. Delighted, Irina reported this at home. Her father, who loved music, decided he wanted to meet the boy. So one day Dmitri came home from school with an invitation to visit the Kustodievs.

Mrs. Shostakovich had been lukewarm about the invitation since she did not know the family. But a few days later Irina repeated the invitation and added that her father would be very upset if Dmitri refused. The occasion was not exactly normal, for Kustodiev was seriously ill; he had had two operations and his legs were atrophied. For years he had been confined to a chair and suffered terribly as he worked. Naturally, his family did everything possible to brighten his life, hence the idea of inviting young Shostakovich. In view of all the circumstances, his parents allowed him to go.

Irina Kustodiev later reminisced: "I well remember Dmitri Shostakovich's first visit. A little boy with a shock of hair, he went up to my father, said hello, and handed him a long strip of paper on which his entire repertoire was listed in a neat column. Then he went to the piano and played all the pieces on the list, one after another. The results exceeded all our expectations, and he immediately won father over."

That day saw the beginning of a long and deep friendship between the Kustodievs and the Shostakoviches. Mrs. Shostakovich often took the children to visit the Kustodievs. Knowing the artist's great love of music, she also took along two pupils from Nikolaev's piano class—the outstanding pianists Vladimir Sofronitsky and Maria Yudina. Dmitri played the piano every time he went. Of course he did more than that: there were two children his own age in the house (a boy, Kyril, the same age as Maria Shostakovich, as well as Irina), and they often went off to play happily together.

Kustodiev not only loved music, but also knew a lot about it, and was a fine judge. He talked divertingly of works by Russian composers, and of symphony concerts under Ziloti, Koussevitzky, and other famous conductors he had heard in his youth. He did two pictures of the young Shostakovich. The first was a portrait of the lad holding some music by Chopin (it was given to Shostakovich and is now in the composer's Moscow apartment); the second, a pencil drawing of the boy at the piano, which bears the inscription "Dmitri Shostakovich, May 8, 1920, at my exhibition at the House of Art. B. Kustodiev."

Kustodiev made this drawing when the boy played at the opening of an exhibition of his works. The piano was in one of the rooms where the paintings were being shown, and Kustodiev saw Shostakovich in an unusual pose, sitting with his back to the audience, leaning slightly to the left toward the bass keys. In the Kustodiev apartment the piano stood with the keyboard toward the window, so from his normal position the artist could see only the player's face. Evidently the new pose, full of expression, caught his eye and led him to make the sketch. It was given to Mrs. Shostakovich.

There is a concert program—a memento of Shostakovich's

first performance of his own works, when he played two of his Preludes at a Conservatory concert in 1921—which might be a reply from the young musician to the venerable artist. On it is written, in the composer's hand: "To dear Boris Mikhailovich, in memory of my first appearance before the public playing my own stuff. With love, D. Shostakovich."

Kustodiev undoubtedly left a deep impression on the young Shostakovich through both his personality and his work. The boy often watched the artist at work, noticing what subjects appealed to him and pondering over them. In 1922, while Shostakovich was often at the Kustodievs' house, Kustodiev was commissioned to do the illustrations for *Lady Macbeth of Mtsensk District*. The book came out in 1930, after the artist's death, and it was then that Shostakovich had the idea for his second opera.

As during the composition of *The Nose*, Shostakovich himself began to prepare a libretto. Despite his complete captivation by Leskov's story, he did not intend merely to "add music." Many things, in his view, had to be reworked and accentuated differently.

Leskov, a superb narrator, had written in deliberately un-emotional language about the events in a merchant's family in a small provincial town. He left it to his readers to draw conclusions from the story of how a woman, married off to a man she does not love, becomes a criminal under the influence of awakening passion: first she kills her loathsome father-in-law, then her hateful husband, and finally, urged on by her vengeful lover, a young nephew who stands between her and wealth. Subtly, unobtrusively, Leskov depicts the background to the tragedy—the callousness of a society in which a woman is not recognized as a person or an individual; the deadly boredom of the merchant's home; the unrelieved monotony of a senseless life with nothing to brighten it. Against this background he places a passionate, energetic personality who can express her energy and individuality only through crime.

The title of the work uses a Shakespearean character. This is not an isolated example in Russian literature: the great author Turgenev had called his account of the fate of a provincial dreamer among the intelligentsia *The Hamlet of Shchigrovsky District*, thus indicating ironically his hero's narrow views and limited horizons. A district (*uyezd*) was a small administrative unit in Tsarist Russia. The word did not imply smallness of size only, however, but also distance from the capital and cultural centers, backwardness. In calling his work *Lady Macbeth of Mtsensk District*, Leskov was also stressing this narrowness and cultural poverty.

Shostakovich greatly admired Leskov's heroine, the merchant's wife Katerina. But, as distinct from Leskov, he decided to "dot all the *i*'s": to write a work sympathetic to the criminal, who is in fact a victim of the whole social order in which she lives.

"There is perhaps no more expressive work in Russian literature showing the position of women in the old, prerevolutionary days," the composer wrote in an article entitled "My Understanding of *Lady Macbeth*." He went on to describe his point of view in detail, also setting out the contents of the opera as he conceived it:

> My task was to show that Katerina was entirely justified. . . .
> I excluded the murder of the nephews, which was purely for selfish reasons. . . .
>
> I try to treat Katerina as a positive character who deserves the audience's sympathy. It is not so easy to evoke sympathy: Katerina commits crimes which are not compatible with morals or ethics—two murders. . . .
>
> I would like to explain the action this way. Katerina is a clever, gifted, and attractive woman; because of the nightmarish conditions in which life has put her, and a cruel,

greedy, petty merchant environment, her life becomes sad, uninteresting, and miserable. She does not love her husband, she has no pleasures, nothing to console her. Then along comes Sergei, an assistant hired by her husband. She falls in love with the assistant, an unworthy character, and in that love she finds happiness and a purpose for her existence which she had lacked.

To achieve that purpose . . . she commits a series of crimes.

When Boris—her father-in-law—notices Sergei saying good night to Katerina after a rendezvous and decides to flog him, she is seized with a desire for vengeance and poisons Boris for the suffering he has caused her lover. And when, one day, Sergei tells her . . . he wants to be her husband, she replies that he shall. So when Zinovy returns home after a long absence, she strangles him. . . .

It is not worth discussing how I justify all these things, since they are justified far more by the musical material. I feel the music in the opera plays the main, the leading, the decisive role.

Katerina throws everything into her love for Sergei; nothing outside that love exists for her, and when, after the crimes are discovered, she ends up in the penal colony with Sergei, her accomplice, and when she realizes that he no longer loves her but has fallen in love with Sonetka from the colony, she drowns Sonetka in the river and then drowns herself. . . .

It would be most accurate to call her crimes a protest against the society in which she lives.

Shostakovich began work on the opera at the end of 1930. He began with the libretto, for which he enlisted the help of one of the librettists of *The Nose*, Preis. He could not start on the music, however, until September 1931, when he made his now regular journey to Gudauta. He went there to relax and work in peace, having literally fled from his many tasks. In a letter dated September 1 he wrote: "Dear Ivan Ivanovich, Today I reached Gudauta. Everything is the same. The only bad thing is that it's cold. It keeps raining. . . . Don't tell anyone my address—I left a lot of loose ends in Leningrad." A week later, he wrote: "I've finished Scene 2 of the opera."

The work went well, and he stayed in Gudauta for two months, during which he wrote the entire first act. He spent the end of his vacation traveling in the Caucasus: from Gudauta, on October 26, he left for Batum, arriving by boat on the 28th. He wrote to Sollertinsky: "Dear Ivan Ivanovich, The day after tomorrow I leave for Tiflis. . . . This is to let you know that I've completed the first act of the opera in short score. I'm orchestrating it when not preoccupied with swimming and food."

For the few days he spent in Tiflis, Shostakovich stayed with the Georgian composer Andrei Balanchivadze,* who had graduated from the Leningrad Conservatory and maintained friendly contact with many musicians in the city. There, at Balanchivadze's home, the orchestration was completed and a note added to the manuscript: "End of 1st Act. 5.xi.1931. Tiflis." There too Shostakovich first played the completed fragment to his delighted comrade.

The second act was composed in the winter of 1931–32 in Leningrad, and completed in March while Shostakovich was in Moscow. He decided to take the piece to both Moscow opera houses; both displayed an interest in the work. Heartened by the prospect of performances in two Moscow theaters, Shostakovich started immediately on the third act when he returned to Leningrad. He did not manage to write much, however, for this was the time of a momentous and joyful event—his wedding.

Shostakovich had met his future wife, Nina Varzar, in

---

* Brother of the famous dancer and choreographer, George Balanchine.—Trans.

the summer of 1927, while vacationing and working on *The Nose* in Detskoye Selo, formerly Tsarskoye Selo, near Leningrad. He was living in the Scholars' Resort while two young sisters, Irina and Nina Varzar, had taken rooms with a landlady nearby and went to the Resort for their meals. The sisters spent their spare time together playing tennis in the evenings and walking in the beautiful grounds of the Pushkin Lycée.* The younger sister, Nina, with her dark hair and dark eyes, her femininity, and her exceptional personality, attracted universal attention. Evidently she made a great impression on Shostakovich. In any event their friendship continued after their return to Leningrad, and an interest in the Varzar family can also be detected in Shostakovich's letters from Moscow during the winter of 1927–28.

Five years later, in May 1932, they got married. There was no ceremony or costly celebration. Nina, who had just graduated from the most demanding faculty of Leningrad University and who had taken up the far from feminine profession of experimental physicist, was again holidaying at Pushkino. Shostakovich traveled out to join her and they registered their marriage in the village.

In August, Shostakovich and his young wife went to the Gaspra sanatorium in the Crimea. The summer in the Crimea was very hot, to be sure, and Shostakovich could never bear the heat. A true native of Leningrad, he was happiest in cold, damp weather and preferred rain to sunshine. It was no accident that later, when he had a vast choice of places to relax and work in, he chose Repino, a village outside Leningrad where the Union of Soviet Composers had one of its retreats. But in August 1932, in spite of the mercilessly blazing sun,

---

* A privileged educational institution in Tsarskoye Selo in the nineteenth century. The great Russian poet Pushkin studied there. Today the village where the Lycée stood is known as Pushkino.—Trans.

the stuffy air in their small room, and an abundance of vicious mosquitoes, Shostakovich was unreservedly happy. Never before had he written such cheerful, optimistic letters as he did then, and never, either before or afterward, did he enjoy life so fully and so free from care.

In spite of the honeymoon atmosphere, which would not seem ideally suited to serious work, he did work hard and productively. On August 16 he wrote to Sollertinsky: "Yesterday I finished the third act of *Lady Macbeth*!"

Dmitri Tsyganov, the first violinist of the Beethoven Quartet, was staying at the same sanatorium. Both musicians took part in a concert arranged for the guests. Shostakovich played a piano arrangement of his First Symphony, while Tsyganov played several miniatures for violin, including his own arrangements of pieces for other instruments. Shostakovich was particularly interested in these transcriptions. Later he willingly gave Tsyganov permission to make transcriptions of some of his piano preludes. From then on, his chamber music career was closely linked with the Beethoven Quartet.

The Shostakoviches returned to Leningrad at the end of September. At that time the composer's family was living in Dmitrovsky Passage, lost among the little streets linking Marat Street with Vladimirsky Square. The children had grown up, Dmitri's sisters had moved out of the house and acquired families of their own, and Zoya had even moved to Moscow. Consequently, Mrs. Shostakovich had decided that a modest three-room apartment would be quite adequate for herself and her son. Her bedroom, Dmitri's room, and a living room were all they had in 1932. It was to this apartment that Shostakovich returned with his wife. They lived there until the Union of Soviet Composers, founded in 1932, provided them with more comfortable accommodations on Kirovsky Prospekt, in one of the best sections of Leningrad.

There, in the fall and early winter, the composer completed *Lady Macbeth of Mtsensk District,* dedicated to Nina Shostakovich. On the last page of the score, now preserved in the Central State Archive of Literature and the Arts, is written: "End of fourth act. End of opera. December 17, 1932. D. Shostakovich. Leningrad."

Shostakovich gave his opera the paradoxical description of "tragic satire." And indeed, the unfolding of Katerina's tragedy is organically bound up with satire, the revelation of the loathsomeness of life around her.

The opera's heroine is Katerina Izmailova. The composer devotes the most intense and beautiful pages of the work to her, characterizing her in a number of passages showing each and every aspect of her personality: the dreamy and thoughtful romance "Once I saw through the window"; the bitter reflection on her unjust but "honorable" position in the quasi-majestic passage "I am a merchant's wife, married to the eminent merchant Izmailov"; the proud speech, full of dignity and feeling, in praise of Russian women in the second scene; her cries, filled with anguish and horror, in the scene where her father-in-law cruelly flogs Sergei. But when the murder occurs, the music alters sharply: shrill, vulgar lines and coarse motifs appear. Only at the end, when the criminal's soul is purged after agonies of conscience and jealousy, does the music well up in astonishing beauty, profundity, and power.

The remaining characters in the opera are painted by the music with merciless satire in the broken, angular lines of grotesque scherzos, banal vocal snatches, parodied waltzes, drinking songs, and sentimental romances. In the finale, other colors appear. Here there is tragedy mixed with heroism. Here, for the first time, ordinary people appear, suffering and in chains. The prisoners' chorus "Oh, the road where our chains have dragged" and the song of the old convict are simple, deep, and sorrowful, with true epic greatness.

The opera was accepted first in Moscow at the Nemirovich-Danchenko, and then in Leningrad at the Maly. In addition to a performance at the Bolshoi Theater, which was temporarily postponed, there were plans to put it on in Sverdlovsk, the major industrial center in the Urals. Shostakovich went there on April 9; the next morning he wrote: "I play through *Lady Macbeth* tonight at 7. The local paper, the *Uralsky Rabochii* (Urals Worker), reported my arrival and the fact that I'll 'perform the text of the opera at the piano' on the 10th, at 7 in the evening."

In his next letter three days later, he reported: "On the evening of the 10th I played through *Lady Macbeth*. The theater management gave it a very good reception. Later I played excerpts for the orchestra. Again, a good reception."

On his return journey, staying in Moscow for a few days, the composer wrote: "It was good to hear the first act of *Lady Macbeth* with the orchestra and singers." In other words, work in Moscow was going quickly and well. Leningrad was not far behind. The premières took place almost simultaneously—on January 22, 1934, in Leningrad and on January 24 in Moscow.

The two productions were completely different. Nemirovich-Danchenko, working from the literary source, re-created Leskov's images on the stage. Samosud and the producer for the Bolshoi, Smolich, staging the work in Leningrad, paid more attention to the score and worked on the basis of Shostakovich's handling of the text.

Discussion raged about both productions, with critics crossing swords ferociously in defense of one or the other. Shostakovich, with his usual tact, tried to pacify the antagonists. Meditating on the special problems of opera production, opera singers' acting abilities, and the role of the artist in an article entitled "Thoughts on Musical Drama" published in *Sovyetskoe Iskusstvo* (Soviet Art), he wrote:

I have often wondered . . . which version of *Katerina Izmailova**—Nemirovich-Danchenko's or Smolich's—I prefer. I
find myself in a quandary, since it turns out that I like them
both, but for different reasons. Nemirovich-Danchenko has
brought all the theatrical resources of the Arts Theater sys-
tem† to bear, and in some places his talents have produced
results which literally shook me. But at the same time I felt
that in some places Vladimir Ivanovich‡ was working more
from Leskov's story than the opera libretto. Smolich, on the
other hand, put his profound knowledge of the nature of
opera into his production, and the musical aspect is of the
highest quality.

The opera ran successfully in Moscow and Leningrad for
almost two years. It also aroused interest abroad: the London radio played extracts, and performances were given in
the United States, Sweden, Denmark, and Czechoslovakia.
Critics spoke of the opera's great qualities, and newspaper
articles blazoned headlines like "A Triumph for Soviet
Music," "The Conquests of Soviet Musical Thought," and
"A Brilliant Opera."

Sollertinsky wrote: "One can state with absolute sincerity
that, since the *Queen of Spades*, there has been no work in
the history of Russian musical drama of the scale and depth
of *Lady Macbeth of Mtsensk District.*" Without knowing of
Sollertinsky's verdict, Mordvinov, the producer in Moscow,
repeated it almost word for word: "We have probably not
seen such a monumental composition since the appearance of
the *Queen of Spades.*" And in the course of a nation-wide
broadcast of the Moscow première, Nemirovich-Danchenko
declared: "Shostakovich's music shows genius in its vividness

---

* The opera was named after the heroine in the Moscow production.
Later Shostakovich himself preferred this title.—Trans.
† The so-called Stanislavsky system.
‡ Nemirovich-Danchenko.

and variety of rhythms, its enormous spirit, deep lyricism, and astonishing wealth of orchestral color."

At all events, both productions were a huge success. The opera-going public took up Shostakovich's masterpiece with enthusiasm. People were heard to talk of the composer's genius. And it was not only the critics and audiences who praised the productions highly. While work on the opera was still in progress at the Nemirovich-Danchenko theater, it was given in concert performance for Bubnov, the people's Commissar for Education, and Arkadiev, the chief of the Arts Division. An edict from the Director of the Leningrad State Theaters, calling *Lady Macbeth of Mtsensk District* an important event in the development of Soviet Musical Theater, was issued in Leningrad after the première.

The composer's plans expanded. Not content with *Lady Macbeth* alone, he thought of writing an operatic trilogy, perhaps even a tetralogy, linked by a single theme—the fate of Russian women in various historical periods up to and including the Revolution. This idea was not, however, to become a reality.

[1935–1941]

The year 1935 arrived. In April Shostakovich, along with a large group of Soviet artists including the singers Valeria Barsova and Maria Maksakova, the violinist David Oistrakh, ballet dancers Natalia Dudinskaya and Asaf Messerer, and Lev Oborin, the pianist with whom Shostakovich had long been friends, went on a performance tour of Turkey. The journey proved very wearing, with constant moves from place to place and frequent concerts at which Shostakovich appeared as a pianist playing his own compositions.

In his letters to Sollertinsky, Shostakovich mentioned the music he was playing—all pieces he had written since completing the opera. These included, first, the twenty-four piano Preludes, a collection reflecting the influence of his beloved Chopin and, like Chopin's Preludes, in all twenty-four keys. They were varied in character. Some passages in the *Mazurka*, the *Nocturne*, and the *Funeral March* echoed well-known Chopin pieces re-created in pure Shostakovich style, while others were the result of his observations and exercises in different moods.

The Preludes had been composed very quickly, at the rate of one a day, their dates recorded by the composer. The first was written on December 30, 1932, the second the following day, and the third on January 1, 1933; more followed on January 4, 5, 7, and 11. They represent a veritable mine of invention in which great treasures are mingled with lesser happy touches. Perhaps the finest are the lyrical movements, bright and poetic.

A little later in 1933 Shostakovich had written his Piano Concerto. Again, various sides of the composer's musical imagination came into play. The four movements demonstrate a remarkable blend of lyricism with a caustic cancan, and of echoes from seventeenth-century music with the lively din of modern streets and squares. Shostakovich makes use of quotations from Bach, Beethoven, Weber, and Haydn, recreating them with good-natured humor and sometimes biting sarcasm. Only the second movement, in the style of a slow waltz, stands out for its deeply felt lyricism. It too contains a quotation, but a serious one without parody: the expressive theme from the final adagio—the sixth movement —of Mahler's Third Symphony.

Shostakovich had already "baptized" the concerto: before the Turkish tour began he performed it in Leningrad with the Philharmonic under Stiedry. According to those who heard that performance, he gave an arresting interpretation, playing with great conviction and literally "making the audience listen." Then he completed his next work, the Sonata for Cello, in which he revealed himself as a deeply and poetically sensitive lyric musician, immediately before the tour.

Shortly after he returned from the tour, on December 26, 1935, *Lady Macbeth of Mtsensk District* was given another première on the auxiliary stage of the Moscow Bolshoi Theater. Almost simultaneously the Leningrad Maly Opera Theater, which had brought Shostakovich's opera to perform, began a season in the capital. As a result, *Lady Macbeth* could be seen in the capital in three theaters at once.

The very next day, however, *Pravda* appeared with an editorial entitled "Chaos, Not Music," criticizing Shostakovich's opera. Returning to Leningrad in early March, Shostakovich again found himself criticized in connection with the *Pravda* article; he was accused of formalism, naturalism, and breaking with reality.

Stormy debates on Shostakovich's music took place within the Union of Composers at the Maly Opera. Some voices were raised in defense of the composer and his work. At one discussion the composer Mikhail Chulaki said: "Personally, I liked *Lady Macbeth*. I still do. I can't imagine how some comrades, after an article in *Pravda*, can say, 'No, I don't like it anymore,' when they haven't even listened to it a second time!" Shostakovich himself fell to thinking very deeply: he took serious and careful note of the critical remarks.

His friends were a great source of support during this difficult period. Shostakovich had long enjoyed a warm relationship with Marshal Tukhachevsky, the outstanding Soviet military commander. A talented regimental officer and a man of great refinement and varied interests, Tukhachevsky was also an accomplished amateur musician who always kept abreast of musical events. In 1925, hearing of the gifted youth who was writing a symphony, he had asked some mutual acquaintances to bring Shostakovich to see him when he was in Moscow. Over the ensuing years the composer visited Tukhachevsky when he was in the capital, and played him his new compositions. Together with Oborin and Bryushkov, he had also visited Tukhachevsky before leaving for the Chopin competition. The musicians had each played in turn, and Tukhachevsky had listened attentively, occasionally making quiet, tactful, and pertinent comments. He had also rendered Shostakovich great practical assistance: "I remember being summoned unexpectedly to see Shaposhnikov, the commander of the Leningrad military district," the composer wrote in "How I Miss Him," his memories of the Marshal. "Tukhachevsky, it turned out, had phoned him from Moscow. He had heard of the difficulties I was in, and asked that I should receive help on the spot. And I did."

When he heard *Lady Macbeth of Mtsensk District*,

Tukhachevsky appreciated its true worth. Samosud, who conducted the opera in Leningrad, passed on what the Marshal said to him: "This tragedy will become the first classic Soviet Opera. One cannot grasp all its strengths at one hearing."

Tukhachevsky displayed touching concern for Shostakovich after the blow he had suffered. "I met him [Shostakovich], crushed and distraught, at the Tukhachevskys' apartment," a close friend of the Tukhachevsky family recalled. "You should have seen how sympathetically Tukhachevsky treated him! They went off together into his study for a long while. I don't know what they talked about, but when Shostakovich came out he was a new man. He went determinedly over to the piano and started to improvise. Tukhachevsky was all ears. He didn't shift his gaze from his friend: he had faith in Shostakovich, and could make him have faith in himself."

Meyerhold's behavior was also touching. Relations between him and Shostakovich had changed since they had first met. Originally the older man had shown attention and concern, and the younger, deep admiration. Later, when they got to know each other better, while Shostakovich was living with Meyerhold in Moscow and working in his theater, disagreements and mutual unease had developed, as is inevitable when two such strong and different personalities live together.

Meyerhold was a very difficult person. Literally all his close associates remembered this and spoke of him as "uncompromisingly continental." No doubt this also affected Shostakovich, who was reserved, shy, and delicate, but had a sharp eye and could accurately observe failings and mock them viciously. He was not sparing in his imitations, giving free rein to irony and even sarcasm, and there was always material to work with. Whole pages of Shostakovich's letters, dating both from when he was living in Moscow and from later short trips to the capital, are devoted to Meyerhold. This alone indicates that the gifted producer occupied his thoughts a good deal, although relations between them were sometimes strained.

In reply to a letter from Shostakovich, Meyerhold wrote in the fall of 1936:

> I was very upset to learn you don't feel well. My dear friend, be brave! Be strong! Do not give in to your sadness!
>
> Stiedry tells me that your new symphony is to be performed soon in Leningrad. I'm doing everything I can to be in Leningrad for that concert. I'm convinced that when you hear your new composition you'll rejoin the battle for new, monumental music, and that your ire will turn to ashes in the midst of your renewed endeavors.
>
> I greatly look forward to seeing you and talking with you!

The new symphony to which Meyerhold referred was the gargantuan Fourth, written at the end of 1935 and the beginning of 1936. But the producer could not attend the première —it was given thirty years later! Not long before the day of the concert, Shostakovich was obliged to call it off.

Shostakovich worked on the Fourth Symphony during the storm surrounding *Lady Macbeth of Mtsensk District*. In a letter to Andrei Balanchivadze, he said: "I'm now finishing the 4th Symphony. The composition part is done, and I'm now orchestrating. I think I'll be done in a week, since the music doesn't come to me much before the orchestration."

A few days later, on April 17, Shostakovich wrote to Shebalin in Moscow: "As for me, I've almost finished my symphony. I'm now orchestrating the finale (3rd movement). When I finish I'll come to Moscow if I can, to show it to you and one or two other people. I'm very bitter. I don't know what to do next, so I'm dragging out finishing the symphony. Working steadily I could finish it in about five days, but since I'm not doing very much, it'll take ten or fifteen. Basically, nothing has changed."

The symphony was an enormous task: a gigantic three-movement structure with a first movement lasting more than twenty-five minutes. Shostakovich began to write it on September 13, 1935; its completion is dated May 20, 1936. The concept of the work proved that Shostakovich had embarked on genuine symphonic writing in the purest and deepest sense of the term. After the superficially dramatic one-movement Second and Third Symphonies the composer, enriched by the experience of his opera, now started for the first time to create a philosophical, tragic symphonic cycle.

The fact that Sollertinsky had in his own good time introduced him to the works of Mahler and infected him with his boundless love for this unique humanist and artist was highly significant. Sabinina, the author of a thoughtful and sensitive study of Shostakovich's symphonies, writes:

> The Fourth is the most "Mahlerian" of Shostakovich's symphonies. It would be incorrect, however, to look for links between Shostakovich and Mahler only in their language . . . and compositional details—the sudden and seemingly similar contrasts representing the gulf between the internal world of the artist and humanist, and the aggressive banality of his surroundings. The "Mahlerian," in the deepest sense of the word, lies in his approach to the problem of "the individual and the surrounding world," his attempts to expose fully the contradictions in life which torment him.

It is stated above that Shostakovich began the symphony on September 13. The score says so, and this date has entered the musicological literature on Shostakovich. But the idea of the symphony had matured significantly earlier— perhaps not even just the idea, but also specific details of its execution which, as always, he would have discussed with his closest friends. Otherwise how could Sollertinsky, speaking at a discussion of Soviet symphonic writing on February 5 and 6, 1935, say: "I await the emergence of Shostakovich's Fourth Symphony with great interest. I believe this work will be a far remove from the three symphonies Shostakovich has written up to now."

The Leningrad Philharmonic Orchestra under Stiedry was already rehearsing the symphony when Shostakovich put off the performance. He gave as his reasons the fact that he could see glaring defects in the work and considered it a failure. But this was not the case at all. The Fourth Symphony contains wonderful music, as confirmed by its hugely successful reception in 1962, when it was at last performed in concert. The imposing symphonic structure is perhaps one of Shostakovich's greatest creations. But too much in it could have invited reproof in 1936, and he did not want to take the risk.

He did allow the public to judge his next symphony, the Fifth, which was first performed in the Great Hall of the Leningrad Philharmonic on November 21, 1937. Yevgeni Mravinsky conducted.

"I was still an unknown young conductor," Mravinsky recalled years later, "when I was suddenly given Shostakovich's Fifth Symphony, which he had only just completed, to prepare for the celebrations of ten years of Soviet music. To this day I cannot understand how I dared take on such a proposition without great trepidation and reflection. . . . My excuse is that I was young and did not realize the difficulties that lay ahead or the enormous responsibility I had been given. Besides, I was counting on help from the composer."

Together with information on the performance of the symphony, in 1937 the Leningrad young people's paper *Smena* (Shift) printed an article by Mravinsky entitled "A Work of Staggering Force":

This symphony is, I consider, a phenomenon of world-wide significance. It has staggering strength and depth of philosophical conception embodied in strict forms which are classical in their simplicity and greatness.

The complete mastery of the writing is so obvious that it does not require any comment. . . .

I can only compare my feelings as the first musician to perform this symphony with what I experienced when coming into contact with the finest examples of the world's musical literature.

The symphony was brilliantly performed, exactly as the composer had conceived it, and had a glowing, rapturous reception. The papers carried articles not just by music critics but also by ordinary music lovers, among them the eminent author Alexei Tolstoy and the renowned flier Mikhail Gromov.

Naturally, there were also critical views and disapproving articles. Some people found the music full of thick, gloomy colors, pathos, and suffering brought to a naturalistic shriek; in the third movement they saw dread numbness and shades of morbidity. But another point of view, expressed by Alexei Tolstoy, who must have sensed that the symphony and its composer would be challenged, prevailed: "'We dismiss without appeal the criticism by some comrades that Shostakovich's Fifth Symphony is too serious, because such criticism belongs to those who are incapable of great and serious works." His article reads like a fulsome toast: "Before us stands the great realistic art of our time. . . . It is a credit to our age that we can produce such treasures of sound and ideas in abundance. It is a credit to our people that it brings forth such artists."

After the symphony was performed in Moscow, one of the Soviet Union's major musical figures, Heinrich Neuhaus, voiced his impressions: "Deep, meaningful, gripping music, classical in the integrity of its conception, perfect in form and the mastery of orchestral writing—music striking for its novelty and originality, but at the same time somehow hauntingly familiar, so truly and sincerely does it recount human feelings."

A few days previously, before the Moscow première, an article by Shostakovich entitled "My Artist's Reply" had appeared. In it the composer wrote:

> The birth of the Fifth Symphony was preceded by a protracted period of internal preparation. Perhaps because of this, the actual writing of the symphony took a comparatively short time (the third movement, for example, was written in three days). . . .
>
> The theme of my symphony is the development of the individual. I saw man with all his sufferings as the central idea of the work, which is lyrical in mood from start to finish; the finale resolves the tragedy and tension of the earlier movements on a joyous, optimistic note.
>
> We are sometimes faced with the question of whether tragedy is even a legitimate genre in Soviet art. Here, however, genuine tragedy is often confused with resignation and pessimism. I think Soviet tragedy as a genre has every right to exist. But the contents must be suffused with a positive inspiration like, for instance, the life-affirming pathos of Shakespeare's tragedies. We also know of many masterpieces in musical literature where the stern, inspirational language of Verdi's or Mozart's Requiem can fill the human soul not with weakness and despair, but courage and the will to fight.

How, one wonders, did the composer arrive at such a concept of an intense symphonic tragedy? Sollertinsky's words, spoken during the stormy discussions of *Lady Macbeth of Mtsensk District* in 1936, come to mind: "His main weakness is the lack of truly heroic inspiration, and he must work very hard in the fields of both heroic opera and the heroic symphony. . . . I think he should take up Soviet musical tragedy and the Soviet heroic symphony." His friend's advice must indeed have meant a great deal to Shostakovich, since the first work he wrote (excluding film music) after these words was a symphony—and what a symphony!

But the article just quoted here started arguments about the underlying concept of the symphony which have not been settled to this day. Some researchers maintain that the symphony is subjective and individualistic in content, and refer for evidence to Shostakovich's words about the development of the individual and about man with all his sufferings, explaining that these are the composer's own sufferings and that the symphony is autobiographical. Others reject this point of view. Thus the academician Asafyev reflected: "This unsettled, sensitive, evocative music which inspires such gigantic conflict comes across as a true account of the problems facing modern man—not one individual or several, but mankind."

The composer himself, in a conversation with the author Chingiz Aitmatov at the end of the 1960s, said: "There are far more openings for new Shakespeares in today's world, for never before in its development has mankind achieved such unanimity of spirit: so when another such artist appears, he will be able to express the whole world in himself, like a musician."

"The whole world in himself"—does not this one phrase contain the answer to all the researchers' speculations? Of course Shostakovich wrote the Fifth Symphony about himself. If we recall the time when it was written and the details of Shostakovich's life, we too will hear his story in the tragedy of the first movement with its tortured turbidity and yearning; in the humor of the scherzo with its apparently simple jollity which, however, is pervaded by subtle, mocking irony; and in the deep meditation of the largo where everything extraneous, incidental, and transitory is set aside, leaving the hero of the symphony alone with his fears and doubts and questionings. The finale brings a resolution to these problems, but it is by no means a final victory; many difficult trials still lie ahead. But the past has been overcome, and the hero looks to the future with a firm and resolute gaze.

Even if we knew nothing about the composer, the symphony would still grip us, for it goes wider and deeper than Shostakovich's personal pain and suffering. Hearing the symphony, we know it is about us and our complicated, ambiguous age, which can still overcome all and move resolutely onward to light and happiness.

Many things had changed in the composer's life by the time the Fifth Symphony was premièred. A year before, in 1936, he had become a father: his daughter, whom they named Galina, was born in May. Their apartment on Kirovsky, which had been cozy for two, now seemed small. They exchanged it for another one in the vicinity, again on the Petrograd side. There Shostakovich wrote all his subsequent compositions, including the Seventh Symphony. As always, he was working on several pieces at once: the music for Afinogenov's play *Hail, Spain!*, commissioned by the Pushkin Drama Theater in Leningrad, as well as film music and songs to poems by Pushkin.

In May 1938 the Shostakoviches had a son. They named him Maxim, after the husband of one of Dmitri's aunts, Maxim Kostrikin, a communist who had been hidden by the Shostakovich family in the anxious years before the Revolution. Kostrinkin, cheerful, vivacious, and committed, had made a deep impression on Dmitri as a boy.

In the summer of 1938 Shostakovich wrote his First String Quartet. It was his second excursion into chamber music, following the 1934 Cello Sonata. With his customary humor he reported in a letter to Sollertinsky, who was in a hospital:

"I've finished . . . the quartet . . . I played the beginning for you. It got changed around during composition: the first movement is now the last and vice versa. There are four movements altogether. It didn't come out dead right; but then, it's hard to compose well. It takes skill."

Shostakovich was not yet deeply committed to the quartet as a genre. He confessed: "I began to write it [the First Quartet] without any particular idea or feeling in mind, and thought nothing would come of it. The quartet is one of the hardest musical mediums. I wrote the first page as a sort of exercise in quartet form, without any thought of completing it. But then the piece took hold of me and I completed it very quickly. One shouldn't look for any great depth in this first quartet. I'd call it a 'springtime' work."

The First Quartet was a great success with the public. The Leningrad-based Glazounov Quartet performed it, and then the Beethoven Quartet took it up. This first encounter of the Beethoven Quartet with Shostakovich's music involved an amusing misunderstanding. The quartet parts arrived a few days before the composer did, and the players immediately got down to learning them in accordance with the composer's markings. When they played the work to Shostakovich, however, it turned out that all their tempos were wrong, although the composer had inserted metronome marks everywhere and the performers had scrupulously observed them. Finally it was discovered that Shostakovich had set the tempos using his watch, which was broken. Shostakovich was very embarrassed and spent a long time apologizing. This incident in no way clouded relations between Shostakovich and the Quartet, however. He subsequently commissioned them to première all his quartets, which he composed with an eye to the group and the individual characters of each of its members.

During work on the First Quartet, the players had the idea of performing with Shostakovich rather than just performing his compositions, and asked him to compose a piano quintet. He replied, "I'll write a quintet immediately, and I'll definitely play it with you." The première of the Quintet for Piano and String Quartet took place a year later. It was a clear, poised classical work, reminiscent of the refined language of Bach, and won its listeners over with its austerity, balanced proportions, and wise simplicity.

The quintet was the first piece to win Shostakovich the highest honor of the period—the Stalin Prize. This honor was first given to artistic figures in 1940, and was conferred upon very few—the crème de la crème—among whom Dmitri Shostakovich took his rightful place. It was an acknowledgment of his services to the country's musical development and of the size and range of his talents.

Since Shostakovich's youth, Moussorgsky had had a place of honor among his favorite and most admired composers. Shostakovich had always loved his music. "I'm passionately fond of Moussorgsky, a man I revere and esteem," he once wrote. To a certain extent, he followed the same course as Moussorgsky with his operas. Moussorgsky's unfinished comic opera *The Wedding* was based on a comedy of the same name by Gogol. In the last act of *Lady Macbeth*, perceptive listeners could clearly identify the tradition of Moussorgsky's folk-music dramas.

The fate of Moussorgsky's compositions on stage had been a complicated one. *Boris Godunov* was rewritten several times in accordance with the demands of the Tsarist Theater Committee. After Moussorgsky's death his friend Rimsky-Korsakov, desiring unselfishly to see *Boris* performed on stage, made his own version of the opera and reorchestrated it. What the opera gained in elegance, however, it lost in individuality and elemental force. Attempts were made to resurrect the composer's own version of the opera, but Moussorgsky's orchestration, despite its rich colors, suffered from certain inadequacies that prevented the work from revealing its true strength.

At the end of the 1930s Samosud, then head conductor of the Bolshoi Theater, decided to stage *Boris* in a new, more restrained orchestration, which the theater management turned to Shostakovich to provide. Shostakovich accepted willingly, although he was well aware of the difficulty and responsibility of the task facing him: he had to preserve the composer's conception intact, literally transforming himself into Moussorgsky and abandoning his own distinctive orchestral approach. And so the great task began. While it was in progress, discouraging news arrived: the Bolshoi had changed its principal conductor; the musician replacing Samasud had drawn up completely different plans, in which *Boris Godunov* had no place. Nonetheless, Shostakovich continued with the reorchestration: he could not abandon what he had begun. The new version was completed in the summer of 1940. The première took place almost twenty years later, in 1959, at the Kirov Theater in Leningrad.

Shostakovich had long dreamed of creating a musical portrait of Lenin, whom he had admired since childhood, when the events of the 1917 Revolution had unrolled before his inquisitive and impressionable eyes. The desire to write a symphony dedicated to Lenin was born, as Shostakovich himself stated, in 1924, during the dark days when working men the world over wept at the death of the founder of the first proletarian state. Back then, however, Shostakovich had not felt sufficiently confident to implement his grand design. During the 1930s he made several starts, and in 1938 the press announced that he had begun work on a grand symphony for soloists, chorus, and orchestra in memory of Lenin. Shostakovich proposed to draw on Mayakovsky's poem "Vladimir Ilyich Lenin" and poems by Suleiman Stal-sky, the Dragestan folk poet, and by the Kazakhstanian folk singer and improviser Dzhambul. "The fundamental text is the Mayakovsky poem," he wrote two years later. "Maya-kovsky's passionate, ardent language provides excellent ma-terial. But the peculiarities of his poetry—his compressed, terse phrases—create considerable problems for a com-poser." Even in 1940, however, the year of the preceding statement, the slow-maturing design was not realized. The solution came to Shostakovich only after another four years, and then at last the symphony dedicated to Lenin was born.

It seems highly probable that the as yet unrealized project had an effect on the character of the majestic and funereal first movement of the Sixth Symphony. It is no coincidence that researchers discover in the thematic material of the first movement a resemblance to the Eleventh Symphony, with its overtones of popular Russian revolutionary songs. The Sixth Symphony was written in 1939, soon after the First Quartet. Everything about the new work came as a complete surprise to its audiences: three movements instead of the usual four; the absence of a fast opening sonata allegro; and the second and third movements, which shared a series of similar images. "A symphony without a head," some critics called it. It was left to time to reveal the vitality, beauty, and superla-tive value of this most musical piece.

In the summer of 1937 the management of the Leningrad Conservatory invited Shostakovich to give classes in special-ist composition and orchestration. Shostakovich hesitated for a long time before consenting, for he did not feel he had a gift for teaching; by nature shy and reserved, he could not imagine how he would fare as a teacher and feared being laughed at. However, everything worked out unexpectedly well. He had no casual students, but students who knew his music and thought highly of it. Some of them wanted to take lessons specifically from him, rather than from just any composer in the Conservatory. They were not much younger than their teacher, and some even appeared older. Shostakovich never stressed the distance between himself and his pupils; on the contrary, he brought an air of equality into the classroom, to the extent that when he gave out an exercise to do—for example, to reproduce from memory part of the score of a well-known classical work, or to orchestrate something—he sat down and did it with them. Yet the distance was always there: his students treated him with great and even pointed respect. He sensed that they liked him immensely and trusted him implicitly.

When he started in 1937, he had only two pupils: Yuri Sviridov and Orest Yevlakhov. Their relationship began when he sat them down at the piano and asked them to play a Mozart symphony with four hands. The result was quite fluent, since both were reasonable pianists, but not very expressive, and it drew forth the gently ironic comment: "You play very neatly, very neatly indeed!"

Shostakovich set great store by a good command of the piano. He maintained that a composer could study the musical literature seriously only if he could read from score with absolute fluency. He himself could read not only piano scores of any degree of difficulty, but also the most complex orchestral scores.

His teaching was particularly well organized. He never wasted time, devoting his energies completely to his work and spending hours poring over a student's compositions. At the outset, of course, he had no strictly worked out teaching method, but his wonderful musical sense, unimpeachable memory, impeccable compositional technique, and sense of style rendered his comments priceless. Easily spotting the weakest points in his pupils' essays long before they were complete, he altered them with a few short strokes that made the work unrecognizable: the form took on new grace and the development new sense. Further, his remarks were always meticulous and accurate; he illustrated his advice with examples from the classical literature, brilliantly performed on the spot.

The class gradually grew to include Igor Boldyrev, Yuri Levitin, Abram Lobkovsky, and Venyamin Fleishman. After a while another four students appeared, including a very young but extremely gifted girl called Galina Ustvolskaya. In class the students listened attentively to Shostakovich's comments and animatedly discussed what each had written. They worked in different ways, some bringing several pages to every lesson, others less; but all of them worked hard and determinedly. This was a strict requirement on Shostakovich's part, for he felt that any budding composer simply had to compose a great deal so as to be able, while still a student, to try his hand at different genres, choose his path, and become a real professional. He would not tolerate any hint of dilettantism, and instilled the same attitude in his pupils.

The students differed widely in personality, character, and talent, so that things worked differently for each. Fleishman had the greatest trouble composing. He produced a handful of bars—one or two lines of music—every lesson; if there were three, it was considered a great event. Yet he was one of the most talented—everything he wrote was clear and individual. He wrote a one-act opera—*Rothschild's Violin*, after a story by Chekhov, who was one of Shostakovich's favorite authors—which greatly interested the teacher.

Yevlakhov was often in Shostakovich's thoughts. A gifted, serious musician, he was gravely ill: the doctors found he had tuberculosis of the kidneys. His position reminded Shostakovich of his own illness during his years at the Conservatory, which by an odd coincidence had also been tuberculosis. And so, like Glazounov, Shostakovich showed great concern for his pupil, visiting him in the hospital, bringing the brightest figures in the Leningrad medical world to him for consultations, and helping him obtain a pass to one of the finest sanatoriums in the Crimea. When the young man, who also had recently married a student, proved to have practically no money, Shostakovich put on a bit of a show: he brought him a substantial sum of money and a piece of paper stating that the money had been provided by the social welfare bodies at the Conservatory. He asked Yevlakhov to keep an account on the paper of the money received, for "book-keeping purposes." Only when Yevlakhov came back cured after several months at the sanatorium and went to thank the leaders of the union for their help, did he discover that the money had come from his teacher.

Shostakovich's classes were long; no one worried about the time. Often, after the compositions had all been considered and discussed, they would settle down to play the piano four-hands: the symphonic literature from Mozart and Haydn to Stravinsky, and orchestral works in other genres. Where there was no four-hand transcription, Shostakovich would make one himself. In this way he introduced his pupils to the adagio from Mahler's Tenth Symphony and Stravinsky's *Symphony of Psalms*. They also played piano music proper. Shostakovich would play Bach, Schubert, and Chopin, explaining the formal details of each work and lingering over particular features of the craftsmanship, harmonic language, and melodic construction.

Shostakovich produced music of every era, type, and style at his lessons, but never his own. The only exceptions took the form of negative examples: occasionally he would play something from the essays of his early childhood, showing "how not to compose." He would analyze the pieces carefully and in detail, explaining what in them was poorly written, unsuccessful, or unconvincing.

His classes lasted until late; then they would all go out together into Teatralny Square and gradually disperse.

There were days in the spring and fall, however, when the lesson finished unusually early and Shostakovich could not be found afterward at the Conservatory; this happened whenever there was a soccer match. Shostakovich was a long-standing and passionate soccer fan, supporting teams from his native Leningrad: first *Dynamo*, later *Zenit* as well. He never missed a single remotely interesting match. He would buy a season ticket and turn up at the game in all weather. In summer he would leave his dacha and walk, or be shaken about in a passing cart under the blazing sun or pouring rain, so as to cover the few kilometers to the railway station and catch the suburban train into Leningrad, just to get to the stadium.

He neatly entered the results of each game in his "scorebook," which he kept all his life. Even without it, however, he retained in his memory all the complex figures connected with the soccer championships. His friends would test him— did he remember, they would ask, how many *Zenit* had won by against Moscow's *Spartak* in the first round in such-and-such a year? He would promptly name not only the score, but who scored and in what minute of the game. His reply could be taken on trust; it always proved accurate.

Shostakovich had a friend of many years' standing because of his love of soccer. In the late 1930s he had once met the Leningrad journalist Arkadi Klyachkin, also an ardent fan, at the stadium, and they had taken to going to matches together. Thanks to his journalistic connections, Klyachkin could get Shostakovich tickets for any match (which was far from easy in the days before television). They sat together.

Shostakovich supported his team strenuously but always kept himself "within bounds": he did not shout or whistle. Superstitious, he made pessimistic forecasts but hoped inwardly that they would not come true. He liked to put a bet on particularly interesting games, but here again, he would bet that his team would lose.

Betting against him was extremely profitable. If his favorite team won and Shostakovich therefore lost, he took his companion out to a restaurant where they celebrated the victory together. If the team lost, however, and it was Klyachkin's turn to buy dinner, Shostakovich would not want to go: he was not in the mood for a fling.

Shostakovich knew many soccer players and was enormously proud of the fact, though not without a touch of self-conscious irony. Once he even invited the complete Leningrad *Dynamo* team to his house for dinner. And when notices appeared in Leningrad advertising the start of courses for referees, the friends both immediately signed up—Shostakovich seriously wanted to be a referee! As things turned out, however, the courses were never held.

Soccer and sporting interests where an excellent relaxation and a vital diversion for Shostakovich, but all his energies were taken up by his music. In this regard there could be no mistake, and it drew other musicians and his students to him. Yuri Levitin, one of those closest to Shostakovich, recalled:

> You would wonder what Shostakovich made of the juvenile efforts we took to class during the years we studied with him. Yet it was often obvious that he was genuinely excited by some absolutely raw piece by a pupil whose only merit was its sincerity.
>
> From this we learned that the only real music is that which reflects the workings of the heart. . . .
>
> Shostakovich's comments as he listened to our efforts were almost never unkind, but we could always tell whether he

liked a new piece or not. If he did, his usually calm, cool eyes immediately changed and shone, to the delight of the fortunate student. But what unrelieved boredom, even distress, showed in those same eyes when he had to listen to some patently unsuccessful creation by a student.

Shostakovich's authority and personal example were extremely important in the class. His pupils strove to emulate and imitate him. Much later, Shostakovich would be accused of "spawning little Shostakoviches," but it was only natural for young musicians—and certainly not just his pupils—to be influenced by him. Lacking a distinct artistic personality, they remained within the tradition he established. Eventually the most talented did find their own way forward, their own individual voices.

Colleagues as well as students showed Shostakovich their music and sought his advice. They always received exhaustive and encouraging counsel. Shostakovich was ever willing to share his thoughts and give advice, which testified to his uncommon gift for teaching.

One musician who went to Shostakovich several times was the composer and pianist Rozanov, the nephew of Shostakovich's old teacher, Professor Rozanova, who had known Shostakovich since his childhood. He noted down his recollections of his meetings with Shostakovich. Here is one extract from his notes:

A large window, and in front of it a long desk piled high with papers.

To the left of the window, a tall eighteenth-century English clock. Mahogany furniture; two excellent grand pianos, keyboards facing the window. On the wall, a portrait photograph of a woman. Two doors—one at the back to the bedroom, the other leading into the small, apparently oval dining room. Dark blue wallpaper. There is a magnificent, cascading crystal chandelier, undoubtedly Russian, eighteenth century.

. . . I took Shostakovich my new children's opera, and played and sang everything as best I could. Shostakovich sat beside me, following the score and playing additional vocal parts here and there, listening and looking at the text very closely and attentively. At last he opened his mouth, and said he had liked many things in it. He spoke of the need, in opera, to return to Verdi's principles, saying that contemporary opera needed to be entirely reconsidered and could not go on in the "old style" with arias and connecting passages, but that Wagner was not right either, with his unrelievedly turgid writing.

On August 20 that same year I visited him again and showed him the short score of a concerto for piano and orchestra. When I finished playing, he said: "That's all very fine, only there are too many notes. Write like the classics did. Only essential notes, necessary sounds—nothing superfluous. Don't overdo it. Look for your own style. Look for your individual personality. To begin with, imitate! Choose a feature and reproduce it. It will come out differently in any case. But only imitate the best models, and always know which they are. Don't imitate Rachmaninov. He's a remarkable and astonishingly talented man, but his imitators have not produced anything worthwhile and never will. Listen carefully when you play Bach, imitate Beethoven. Imitate Stravinsky, not Prokofiev. Incidentally, he's the only one right now who has a pianistic compositional style, and he doesn't write unnecessary notes. Study polyphony, write inventions and fugues. Look at how the old masters wrote. For example, look at Haydn's bass lines, how logical and independent they are, look at the shape of them. When you notice some feature, work it out and understand what the essential idea behind it is, then try to put it to use yourself and think, Does it work? But the main thing is, learn to express what you want to say directly and tersely in the appropriate language. There should be no meaningless music."

[1941–1944]

At the end of May 1941 Shostakovich sent his family off to their dacha, while he remained in Leningrad. The dacha was not far from the city, on the Karelian Isthmus by the Gulf of Finland. The composer usually went out there on Saturdays and remained for the weekend, but on June 21 he did not: an examination had been scheduled for the following day at the Conservatory, and there was an interesting soccer match—two, in fact—involving *Dynamo* and *Zenit*.

At a few minutes to ten on June 22 he climbed the stairs to the Small Hall in the Conservatory. The examination began at ten. No one yet knew that those were Leningrad's last moments of peace. On the borders of the Soviet Union, the war was already raging. There was no soccer match. The composer kept his unused ticket for many years, then gave it to the children who were putting together a museum of the Seventh Symphony at school.

From the very first days of the war, life in Leningrad changed drastically. The inhabitants of the city still did not believe that the enemy could threaten them directly, but the whole atmosphere altered sharply. Every day young men, urgently drafted for the city's defense, left for the front. Those Conservatory teachers and students who had not yet dispersed for the vacation went out to dig trenches at the approaches to the city. Shostakovich was there with the rest, putting all his effort into it so as not to lag behind the others. In the evenings he returned to an empty apartment.

He was worried about his family. For a period he had the children home from the dacha, but the weather became impossibly suffocating and presently he sent them back to the country—this time, however, to the village of Syritsa, south of Leningrad, rather than toward the dangerously close Finnish border.

The evacuation of the city began in July. The artistic and educational institutions together with some research institutes were sent back far behind the lines. As a member of the teaching staff, Shostakovich was offered the chance of evacuation with the Conservatory to Tashkent. He refused. He felt that his place, like any healthy young man's, was at that time in the ranks of those defending their country. He applied to the military command to be sent to the front as a volunteer, but was refused. Then, with other musicians, he resolved to join the civil guard.

Three hundred years ago when, during the interregnum, Russia was without any supreme authority and fell prey to foreign intervention, the entire Russian people rose in support of the regular army. Brigades of peasants, artisans, and townspeople formed and, together with the regular forces, drove the foreign armies from Russian soil. A civil guard had also been formed during the war against Napoleon in 1812. And now, in those days of ill omen for Russia, this heroic tradition was resurrected.

People who by their nature and profession were utterly peaceable—factory workers, teachers, architects and designers, musicians and writers, artists and performers, old people not always in good health, and all those not eligible for service—obeyed the call of their hearts and civic duty, and went to enlist in the civil guard. So Shostakovich, together with his pupil Venyamin Fleishman, went to the civil guard headquarters. Fleishman was accepted, but Shostakovich was again turned down.

So Shostakovich enlisted instead in the fire-fighting squad of his local civil defense force. Whenever there was an air-raid warning he had to keep watch on the Conservatory roof and put out any incendiary bombs. During one practice session his soccer-watching friend Arkadi Klyachkin arrived with a photographer from his paper. Their photographs of the composer in his fireman's helmet and overalls on the roof above Teatralny Square became famous all over the world.

Of course Shostakovich did not for one moment forget that he was a composer. At first, in July, he wrote songs, which were the things most urgently needed. He made arrangements of popular romances and songs for the musical brigades at the front: instead of a piano accompaniment, he wrote one for violin and cello—portable instruments which could be taken to the front. But he gradually became aware of the need to write a large-scale, commemorative work devoted to the events taking place.

In his spare time—normally, when the late evening was turning into the clear, ghostly "white nights" of summer—he walked slowly down the old, achingly familiar avenues, squares, and embankments. Despite its wartime air, Leningrad had an austere new beauty: palaces, bridges, and cathedrals were camouflaged; the gold leaf had been removed from the cupolas and spires of the churches, and the many valuable sculptures which had adorned the city were surrounded with sandbags, covered with boards, or buried underground. Klodtov's famous horses had been removed from the Anichkov Bridge. All this was not exceptional precaution but stark necessity, since Hitler wanted to wipe Leningrad off the face of the earth. For many months, beginning in September 1941, Nazi artillery and planes directed shells and bombs at the Winter Palace (the Hermitage), the Public Library, and other historic buildings just as they bombarded military targets, even though these targets contained some of mankind's most precious artistic treasures.

In August 1941 Shostakovich had made a start on the first movement of his Seventh Symphony. The city was emptying; the evacuation continued throughout July and August. On August 22 Sollertinsky left Leningrad with the Philharmonic. Shostakovich had played him the still incomplete first movement. The friends remained silent; there was nothing more to say.

Several times Shostakovich was offered a chance to leave, but he refused. He did not go with the Conservatory, which was evacuated to Central Asia, or with the Composers' Union. Finally, in late August, he agreed to leave with the Lenin Film Studios, chiefly because of the children. On August 29 he wrote: "Dear Ivan Ivanovich, We'll be leaving for Alma-Ata in about two days. We are all well. I miss you very much. I've finished the first movement of the symphony, the one I showed you before your departure."

However, two days later no one was leaving Leningrad: the day that letter was written, Hitler's forces cut the city's last rail link with the rest of the country. The nine-hundred-day siege had begun.

Hitler wished to raze Leningrad to the ground, to destroy both the city and all its inhabitants. He chose artillery bombardment and aerial attacks, hunger and cold, as weapons against a peaceful population—besieged women, old people, and children. On September 4 the guns roared from eleven o'clock to six at night: the Nazis had started to bombard the city. The first damage and fires were reported, and the first casualties among the peaceful inhabitants. Air-raid warnings occurred several times a day. A house on Bolshoi Pushkarsky Street, right outside Shostakovich's apartment window, was set aflame by an incendiary bomb; he could see the glow all night. And then the most terrible thing occurred: the food dumps, where all the city's supplies were stored, caught fire. A choking, sweet-smelling haze hung over the city for many days, as the specter of famine loomed.

Shostakovich worked on. It was the first time in history that a huge symphonic canvas had been created under such conditions. At the outset the composer thought of introducing words to express more fully all the sorrow, anger, and pain accumulated in his heart, and he almost began to write a text himself. But later he gave up the idea, having found music to express his feelings more strongly than any words.

On September 17 he was asked to speak on the Leningrad radio. The broadcast was nearly spoiled. Shostakovich was already on his way to the studio when the usual bombardment started and he had to sit it out in a shelter; however, he arrived for the broadcast at the last minute. Aroused, he stood in front of the microphone, trying to speak quietly, slowly, clearly.

An hour ago I finished scoring the second movement of my latest large orchestral composition. If I manage to write well, if I manage to finish the third and fourth movements, the work may be called my Seventh Symphony. In spite of the war and the danger threatening Leningrad, I wrote the first two movements quite quickly.

Why am I telling you all this? I'm telling you this so that the people of Leningrad listening to me will know that life goes on in our city. All of us now are standing militant watch. As a native of Leningrad who has never abandoned the city of my birth, I feel all the tension of this situation most keenly. My life and work are completely bound up with Leningrad.

Leningrad is my country. It is my native city and my home. Many thousands of other people from Leningrad know this same feeling of infinite love for our native town, for its wonderful, spacious streets, its incomparably beautiful squares and buildings. When I walk through our city a feeling of deep conviction grows within me that Leningrad will always stand, grand and beautiful, on the banks of the Neva, that it will always be a bastion of my country, that it will always be there to enrich the fruits of culture.

In a little while I shall have finished my Seventh Symphony. At the moment the work is going quickly and easily. My ideas are clear and constructive. The composition is nearing completion. Then I shall come on the air again with my new work and wait anxiously for a fair and kindly appraisal of my efforts.

That evening some musicians came to his house on Bolshoi Pushkarsky Street, and he played them his newly completed piece. He played with great animation, imitating the orchestral colors and skillfully highlighting the outlines of the structure. He could sense that the music had gripped his intent audience.

Being professionals, they immediately comprehended the unusual conception of the first movement: the absence of the usual juxtaposition of contrasted themes in the sonata-form exposition, and the sharp conflict between the exposition and the development, in which appeared an image of menace, of an alien force swelling into something enormous, inhuman, and destructive. They seemed to see before them a re-creation of the events taking place. The opening of the symphony portrays Russia, beautiful and blooming and at peace; then the ominous clatter of a military drum suddenly breaks through the bright contented music, and the enemy's dreadful invasion machinery is already on the move. The noise grows, there are screeches, squeals, and roars everywhere. In the gigantic battle scene—not a fight for survival but the destruction of two worlds—relief comes at last. The "peacetime" themes reappear, but they have changed: they are twisted by pain and suffering and now sound a tragic note.

The impression was overwhelming. When the music ended they all sat in silence for a long while. Words seemed out of place, impotent. Suddenly an air-raid warning sounded. They should have gone to the shelter, but no one moved: they wished to hear the piece again. Shostakovich excused himself and went out to take his wife and children to the shelter, then came straight back and began playing the piece again.

He also played the second movement, which is spectral and fleeting, but sensed that his friends had not grasped it as well: they were still under the spell of the first movement, like a gigantic shadow stretching far away. Then the alarm ended. The friends dispersed and Shostakovich returned to the shelter to help his wife get the sleeping children back into the apartment and their beds. The night was over; it was September 18.

One week later, on the 25th, he was thirty-five. Ration cards had long been issued, and the quotas for bread, meat, grain, and fat were reduced twice during the month. People grew weaker daily from lack of nourishment, but the composer worked on, writing the third movement of the symphony. They decided to celebrate his birthday with their few friends remaining in Leningrad. Someone unearthed a bottle of vodka, another had some crusts of black bread laid by, and the Shostakoviches still had potatoes.

A week after that, on orders directly from the City Defense Headquarters in Smolny, Shostakovich and his wife and children were flown to Moscow. Shostakovich agreed to go only because of the children: he realized that they would die in the blockaded city. Immediately upon arriving in Moscow he began trying to get sent back to Leningrad. He had left practically without baggage, taking with him only the score of *Lady Macbeth of Mtsensk District* and the Seventh Symphony. But he was not permitted to return: Leningrad was too dangerous.

On October 15, after a fortnight in Moscow, the composer and his family left the capital bound for the east. The train moved slowly, waiting a long time at each station and section of double track. Supply trains rushed along the single track in the opposite direction, westward, carrying soldiers, food, and medical supplies; on canvas-covered flatcars were things which, judging by the shapes, were tanks and artillery pieces. Overtaking the evacuees' train going eastward went shipments of factory equipment being transported from sites near the front to Siberia, and hospital trains carrying the heavy casualties.

The journey was long enough for a routine to be established. Nina was very busy: at the stops she managed to wash the children's clothes, one of them running to the stationmaster's house to fetch hot water while another set off to get food. Some old friends of the Shostakoviches from Moscow, the composer Vissarion Shebalin and the pianist Lev Oborin, were traveling with them. They passed the time in long conversations and regretted that there was no music to listen to.

It was not until the morning of October 22 that a broad, almost leaden strip, sullen under the stormy fall sky, appeared in front of the train windows: they had reached the Volga. At that point it was about three kilometers wide, and the impression when the train began to cross the bridge was a little unnerving. Those who had been in Leningrad under constant fire, hearing the explosions of bombs nearby, and who had flown by night over the enemy positions to escape, should of course have feared nothing here, but still, involuntarily, they held their breath while the train moved—for an eternity, it seemed—over the Volga; only the steel struts of the bridge moved outside the windows, and they could see leaden ripples and menacing little flecks of foam far below.

Then the train traveled for several hours through a narrow valley which was evidently flooded when the river rose, and again it stopped at stations and sidings. All around were Russian huts and gardens with only women, young and old, to be seen about them. Yet they had an indefinable feeling of being near a major city. They approached the bright ribbon of another river—less broad this time—then another railway bridge, quite small by comparison with the huge structure spanning the Volga, fell behind them, and the train's motion stopped.

Exhausted by the long journey, the unwilling travelers climbed out of the coaches. An enormous, dusty square in front of the station was strewn with people and suitcases, kit bags, bundles, and baskets; tired, pale faces and crying children were everywhere. Some of the others on the train, startled by the sight of a city clearly overflowing with refugees, decided to go on to the Urals and Siberia, but Shostakovich remained. He was concerned about the children, who were exhausted by the long trip, and far from certain that things would prove any better in Sverdlovsk or Perm.

In those difficult days, Kuibyshev really was overflowing. Nazi forces were thrusting savagely toward Moscow, and the government offices, industrial plants, and scientific and cultural institutions had been evacuated from the capital. The People's Commissariats, government authorities, and embassies of the allied and neutral states had all moved to the city on the Volga. The best buildings—old merchant's houses, large apartment buildings constructed under communist rule, and schools—were hastily vacated for them and for countless hospitals. The former inhabitants and the mass of evacuees were billeted on other local residents. Everyone settled down in the cramped space and put up with the inconvenience. But every day more trains arrived from the west and people had to be resettled, fed, and put to work. The city authorities had their work cut out. Yet Shostakovich was immediately allocated what in the circumstances were quite presentable lodgings: a bright, warm room in a handsome building which had once housed expensive furnished rooms. It was, of course, difficult to work in one room with two small and noisy children, but around the beginning of December they moved. They were given a two-room apartment in the same central part of the city, a stone's throw from the Palace of Culture where the Bolshoi Theater, transported from Moscow, was housed. At first their place was almost empty, since the family had flown out of Leningrad with nothing but the bare essentials, but there was a good piano provided by the local music school. There Shostakovich finished the symphony. The finale was completed on December 27, 1941.

Shostakovich desperately wanted his favorite orchestra, the Leningrad Philharmonic, to perform the Seventh, and he wanted Yevgeni Mravinsky to conduct it, as he had the Fifth and Sixth, but they were far away in Novosibirsk. The Bolshoi orchestra began to rehearse the work under Samosud. The première took place on March 5, 1942, and the symphony was repeated in Moscow at the end of the month.

People the world over seized on the performance of the Seventh Symphony as an event of unprecedented importance. The concert was relayed by radio stations in Great Britain and the United States, and acclaim and requests for the score soon began to arrive from abroad. The first foreign orchestra to perform the work was one in London under the direction of Henry Wood. Keen competition for the score developed among the orchestras in the Western hemisphere. Shostakovich's choice fell on Toscanini. Across a world caught in a struggle of unheard-of proportions, an airplane flew from the

U.S.S.R. to the United States bearing an unusual cargo: a box of microfilm containing the score and parts of the Seventh Symphony. It arrived in New York on June 1, and the performing parts were ready on June 25. On July 19 the symphony resounded in one of the studios of New York's Radio City; Toscanini conducted. Almost all the American papers carried reviews of the event. The poet Carl Sandburg, writing in the *Washington Post*, addressed the composer in the following terms:

> All over America last Sunday afternoon goes your Symphony No. 7, millions listening to your music portrait of Russia in blood and shadows. . . .
>
> On a long battle front sagging toward Moscow the Red Army fights against the greatest war machine that ever marched into any country. . . .
>
> The outside world looks on and holds its breath.
>
> And we hear about you Dmitri Shostakovich—we hear you sit there day after day doing a music that will tell the story.
>
> In Berlin no new symphonies, in Paris, Brussels, Amsterdam, Copenhagen, Oslo, Prague, Warsaw, wherever the Nazis have mopped up and made new laws, no new symphonies. . . .
>
> Your song tells us of a great singing people beyond defeat or conquest who across years to come shall pay their share and contribution to the meanings of human freedom and discipline.

Thanks to a heroic effort by the only orchestra remaining in Leningrad and its leader, the conductor Karl Eliasberg, the Seventh Symphony was performed in the besieged city to which it was dedicated. The Leningrad première was an unexampled feat. By the spring of 1942 the entire Leningrad radio orchestra numbered only fifteen. The others had died of starvation or gone, weapons in hand, to defend the city. But the remaining fifteen resolved that the Leningrad Symphony would be performed in Leningrad.

First the orchestra had to be filled out. Posters went up: "All Leningrad musicians please report to the Radio Committee." Efforts were made to seek out those who could not come. "My God, how thin many of them were," one of the organizers of the performance later recalled. "How those people livened up when we started to ferret them out of their dark apartments. We were moved to tears when they brought out their concert clothes, their violins and cellos and flutes, and rehearsals began under the icy canopy of the studio."

A score was sent by one of the transport planes flying medicine to the besieged population. Looking through it, the conductor discovered that the orchestra they had assembled by dint of unbelievable efforts was still too small. So the military command of the Leningrad front released musicians from military units even in the front lines for Eliasberg's orchestra.

The concert took place on August 9, 1942. To prevent artillery fire from interrupting the performance, the commander of the Leningrad front, General Govorov, ordered his batteries to knock out the enemy guns; a special operation, code-named "Squall," was worked out for the purpose. The concert was then broadcast over the Leningrad radio. "Today is a great event in the cultural life of our city," the announcer said before switching to the Philharmonic Hall. "In a few moments you will hear the Seventh Symphony by Shostakovich, our great compatriot, performed in Leningrad for the first time. The very fact that the Seventh Symphony is being performed in besieged Leningrad is a testimony to the indomitable spirit of the people of the city and their pluck, to their belief in victory and their willingness to fight to the last drop of blood to win. Listen, comrades! Now we are switching over to the hall where Shostakovich's Seventh Symphony will be broadcast!" Hearing the announcer's voice, the people on the streets and in their apartments gathered round the loudspeakers. This was their day.

The composer could not but rejoice and feel proud of the symphony's success and the recognition of what it meant, which went far beyond a mere musical event. There was joy within the family also: in mid-March his mother, sister, and nephew finally caught up with him. Emaciated, suffering from dysentery like everyone in Leningrad who had survived the terrible winter under siege, they had been saved thanks to the road over frozen Lake Ladoga—the "road of life." It alone, through all the long winter months, had connected the besieged city with the "mainland." Trucks carrying food moved in an unbroken stream toward Leningrad and returned carrying old people, invalids, and children—anyone who could not help defend the heroic city and had to be saved. Shostakovich could not know that a little girl had left Leningrad by that same route, maybe even at the same time —a little girl called Irina Supinskaya, who just twenty years later would become his wife.

With the arrival of his family, Shostakovich began to feel easier—his worries about them constantly facing mortal danger were over. But he still had friends and pupils behind the enemy front; in these unaccustomed surroundings he missed them and worried about Yevlakhov, who had still not recovered from his serious illness and had been obliged to remain in Leningrad with his old and ailing mother. He was also concerned about the fate of the opera by Fleishman, of whom he knew nothing. Only much later did he learn of the heroic death of his beloved pupil: Fleishman blew himself and a Nazi tank up with a string of grenades. But in the early spring of 1942, Shostakovich wrote to Leningrad: "Dear Orest Alexandrovich, I'm thrilled by you all and your courage and endurance. I'm worried and concerned about Fleishman. I greatly regret not having brought his *Rothschild's Violin* out with me. I could be completing and orchestrating it here. My dear friend, if the piece is at the LSSK [Leningrad Union of Soviet Composers], please do look after it, or better still make a copy and if you have a chance send it to me in Kuibyshev. I dearly love that work and worry lest it be lost."

Shostakovich yearned to go to Novosibirsk. He first got there in the summer of 1942, for the first performance of the Seventh Symphony by his favorite orchestra, the Leningrad Philharmonic, and his favorite conductor, Yevgeni Mravinsky. In Novosibirsk he was in his element and could enjoy the sound of orchestral music, of which he had been deprived for almost a year since there was virtually none in Kuibyshev. In Novosibirsk the Leningrad Philharmonic was giving a glittering season of symphony concerts, playing works by Mozart, Brahms, Mahler, Stravinsky, and Soviet composers. It is not surprising that, while he was in the city, Shostakovich had the idea of moving there with his family. Over the following six months he discussed it seriously in his correspondence with friends, and only in December did it become clear that he would have to give it up. Under wartime conditions it was too complicated to travel so far with an entire family, giving up all they had put together and the life they had created, to venture into the unknown. Novosibirsk could not guarantee him either work or comfortable housing.

In Kuibyshev, on the other hand, he was remarkably well accommodated. Leaving his mother, sister, and nephew in his old apartment, he had moved into another one with four large rooms in one of the best parts of the city. The building, newly constructed and solid, stood high above the banks of the Volga. The view from the upper windows opened onto the river, two and a half kilometers wide, and onto the countryside stretching beyond. His old apartment was close by—

less than half a kilometer—and he could see his mother whenever he wanted.

To Sollertinsky he wrote: "I don't think I'll move to Novosibirsk. It involves too many problems. Here I have a sort of life established. I must say, though, sometimes I find it painfully hard without you, and dull without any music." In spite of this firm decision, his last letter of 1942 contains, along with best wishes for the New Year, the words: "I'm green with envy at not being in Novosibirsk."

Shostakovich's stay in Kuibyshev ended on an unfortunate note: he fell ill with gastric typhoid. Although he was inoculated immediately, he suffered a very heavy attack and was not well for a long time. In May 1943, when his treatment ended, he was sent to Arkhangelskoe, a sanatorium near Moscow; he did not return to Kuibyshev.

After finishing the Seventh Symphony, the composer worked almost simultaneously on three pieces in different genres. Remembering his friends from whom the war had separated him for so long, he set to writing a song cycle, dedicating the six romances on poems by Raleigh, Burns, and Shakespeare to those he considered closest to him. Nina alone among them was with him. The others were all far away: Levon Atovmyan, Meyerhold's former assistant, a musician and active public figure; the old critic Isaac Glikman, once a student of Sollertinsky's and a mutual friend; Sollertinsky himself; and the composers Yuri Sviridov and Vissarion Shebalin.

Rereading Gogol with pleasure during those months, Shostakovich again got an idea from his favorite author and began working on an opera to the full text of Gogol's comedy *The Players*. He enjoyed himself and composed wittily. "It's turning out very well," he told Sollertinsky at the end of November 1942. "I'm orchestrating as I go. I'm afraid I won't finish because I'm too pleased with it." Just a month later he wrote sadly to his friend: "I've made a little progress with my stupid opera. I think I'll soon abandon this senseless chore."

He had plenty of reasons for his pessimistic attitude. One was that the work was growing to a vast size. The prose text, when set to music, became unbelievably long. After writing the first quarter of the opera, Shostakovich discovered that it contained fifty minutes of uninterrupted music. New ideas gradually ousted *The Players* from his mind for good.*

In January, feeling a slight improvement, the composer began to write a piano sonata. "Dear Ivan Ivanovich," he wrote in a letter mailed January 12, "Yesterday I got up for the first time. I spent two hours out of bed. Today three, tomorrow more, and so on. When the pain went away I began working on a sonata for piano. The plan is complete and now I'm writing—slowly."

The illness remained with him for a long time. Only on February 19 did he write: "Dear Ivan Ivanovich, I'm better, and the day after tomorrow I'll start going outside. Yesterday evening Lev Oborin was here. While I was ill I composed the first movement of a sonata for piano. I'm getting down to the second movement. As you can see, I'm working." Shostakovich finished the sonata at the sanatorium at the end of March, and dedicated it to the memory of his beloved teacher Leonid Nikolaev, news of whose death had recently reached him.

In the letter in which he mentioned completing the sonata, he also wrote about his future plans: "I shan't go back to

---

* Eight scenes from the opera, edited by Gennadi Rozhdestvensky, were given their first performance under the latter's direction in the Great Hall of the Leningrad Philharmonic on September 13, 1978, and were recorded.

Kuibyshev, or rather, I don't want to. . . . On my return to Moscow I'll start work at the Moscow Conservatory, where I'm listed as a teacher. . . . So far I have no apartment in Moscow, but I've been promised one. I'm living at the Moscow Hotel, room 430. I don't want to leave Moscow. If the apartment problem gets sorted out I'll bring the children back from Kuibyshev."

This letter is dated March 29, 1943. Less than a month later Shostakovich moved into a new apartment. Gradually life became organized; basic items began to fill the empty rooms. Only after the siege of Leningrad was lifted could the family bring their familiar, comfortable furniture, the pianos, and Shostakovich's desk to Moscow from their old apartment, which had fortunately remained intact. Even before that, however, they managed to establish a routine in somewhat primitive conditions.

Shostakovich spent the summer of 1943 in the Ivanovo Composers' Retreat, northeast of Moscow, and there he composed the Eighth Symphony.

The war was in its third year, and had brought untold tragedy to Russia. The enemy were marching over the Ukraine, burning Byelorussia, ravaging the Baltic region, still squeezing Leningrad in a vise, and shooting entire villages. They had already been pushed back from Moscow and suffered a defeat at Stalingrad, but they were still very strong and with their entire colossal war machine were trying to break and crush the Soviet people. It was obvious that they would fail: the Soviet troops were on the advance, liberating cities, villages, and hamlets from the occupying forces. The Nazi atrocities were revealed to the soldiers: piles of ash and blackened chimneys—all that remained of burned villages; enormous pits filled with bullet-riddled bodies; the concentration camps and death camps with their monstrous industry of destruction. The shocked world learned what the Nazis had hoped to hide from the whole of mankind.

Shock and horror at the barbarousness of Nazism; a deep conviction that such a tragedy—and such a crime against humanity—must never happen again; and the determination to wage war to a victorious conclusion for light and truth on earth—these were the feelings and thoughts embodied in Shostakovich's Eighth Symphony. Being a citizen as well as a composer, and a wonderfully sensitive artist, Shostakovich could not but create a work reflecting the problem of war and peace, war and man at war, war and humanity. The concept underlying the Seventh Symphony, in which he had made a simple contrast of the notions of peace and aggression, now seemed inadequate. He had to use the theme in different ways, on a generalized, philosophical level.

The Eighth Symphony represents the height of tragedy in Shostakovich's output. The realism is relentless, the emotion is stretched to the limit, and there is colossal tension in the expressive means employed. It is an unusual work: the normal proportions of light and shade, tragedy and optimism are disregarded here, while gloomy tones predominate. Among the symphony's five movements, not one brings relief; each is deeply tragic. In spite of its enormous size, the symphony's development is constant and purposeful.

The opening of the first movement sounds a note of warning; a sense of alarm grows until the long buildup of tension culminates in shattering tragedy. The next two movements reveal still more inner energy, and the orchestra becomes deafening in the toccata, where the terrible, unceasing motion seems inhuman. The fourth movement is a majestic and desolate passacaglia. At the beginning of the finale, which follows without a break, light dawns, as if after a long, dreadful night full of fey dreams, the sun has risen.

At the beginning of September, Yevgeni Mravinsky made a

short trip to Moscow from Novosibirsk. When Shostakovich showed him the still uncompleted score, the conductor was thrilled. He resolved to perform the symphony immediately, and took the score with him when he returned to Novosibirsk. He was back in the capital at the end of October, and rehearsals began. Shostakovich was invariably there. He watched as his grand design was transformed into sound under the direction of the sensitive, thoughtful conductor. At one rehearsal, spellbound by Mravinsky's marvelous work, he had the idea of dedicating the symphony to him.

The première of the Eighth Symphony took place in Moscow on November 4, 1943, by which time Sollertinsky had arrived in the capital. Despite the difficulties of wartime, the Soviet Union was observing the fiftieth anniversary of Tchaikovsky's death in grand style, and Sollertinsky had been invited to give the main address at the official meeting of composers and artists. In effect, this was an acknowledgment of his enormous services to Soviet music. The whole country heard his address, for it was broadcast on the radio. On the platform at the meeting, together with other major artistic figures, was Dmitri Shostakovich.

During those few days in Moscow the friends were inseparable. Sollertinsky stayed at the Shostakoviches' spacious but still half-empty apartment, rather than at a hotel. They discussed the latest news avidly. The Red Army was moving steadily forward, liberating more and more areas from the occupying forces; the end of the siege of Leningrad was already in sight; life was returning to normal, and people could think of the future and their long-term plans.

Shostakovich had settled down in Moscow for a long time, but he could not imagine life without his friend. Once again he tried, as he had done in his letters, to convince Sollertinsky to move to Moscow. Another dear friend of his, Shebalin, added his voice to Shostakovich's and, as director of the

Moscow Conservatory, invited Sollertinsky to teach a class there in the history of music. Sollertinsky agreed to give the class, beginning in February 1944.

The friends said good-by at the station. They thought that this time their parting would be a brief one and that after a very short while they would be inseparable again, but this was their last meeting. Sollertinsky managed to make the introductory speech—brilliant as ever—at the première in Novosibirsk of the Eighth Symphony, which was given on February 5 and 6, 1944, but he died on the night of February 10–11. His heart, which had long been under strain owing to serious illness, gave out.

Sollertinsky's death was a terrible blow to Shostakovich. Immediately upon receiving the dreadful news from Novosibirsk, Shostakovich wrote a letter to Sollertinsky's widow:

Dear Olga Pantaleimonovna,

I cannot express in words all the grief I felt when I received the news of the death of Ivan Ivanovich. Ivan Ivanovich was my closest and dearest friend. I owe all my education to him. It will be unbelievably hard for me to live without him. The times kept us apart. In the last few years I rarely saw him or spoke with him. But I was always cheered by the knowledge that Ivan Ivanovich, with his remarkable mind, clear vision, and inexhaustible energy, was alive somewhere. His passing is a bitter blow for me.

Ivan Ivanovich and I talked a great deal about everything. We talked about that inevitable thing waiting for us at the end of our lives—about death. Both of us feared and dreaded it. We loved life, but knew that sooner or later we would have to leave it.

Ivan Ivanovich has gone from us terribly young. Death has wrenched him from life. He is dead, I am still here. When we spoke of death we always remembered the people near and dear to us. We thought anxiously about our children, wives, and parents, and always solemnly promised each other that in the event of one of us dying, the other would use every possible means to help the bereaved family.

Dear Olga Pantaleimonovna, if you are in difficulties, if you have any problems, tell me, I beg you, for the sake of the memory of Ivan Ivanovich which I hold sacred, and if I can help you in any way I shall do my utmost to do so.

If it is not too hard for you, please let me know what Ivan Ivanovich died from. The telegram about his death was of the briefest kind, and it is very important to me to know what happened to him.

I warmly shake your hand, and embrace the poor children.

Yours, D. Shostakovich.

The composer devoutly kept his word given to Sollertinsky's widow at that difficult time. All his life he remembered his friend's bereaved family. He immediately arranged for his young son to receive the maximum pension, and after the siege of Leningrad was lifted he helped the family return to their home.

This was not easy. The war was far from over, the front was not far away, and in Leningrad wartime regulations were being strictly enforced. By no means all of those who wished to enter the city were allowed to do so: special papers were needed. Shostakovich sent an official letter inviting Sollertinsky's widow to Moscow; he met her at the station and put her up at his home, carrying her heavy suitcases from the station himself, since there were no porters or taxis in the city. He arranged all the necessary documents, then put Olga Sollertinsky on the train to Leningrad. Shortly afterward he sent some valuable music to her there—the newly published trio with a touching inscription, not now to his friend as had been his custom, but to his widow.

The trio, written in the spring of 1944, was dedicated to the memory of I. I. Sollertinsky.

In it Shostakovich continued traditions long established in

Russian music. Tchaikovsky had dedicated his trio "to the memory of a great artist"—Nikolai Rubinstein, a wonderful pianist, the first director of the Moscow Conservatory and Tchaikovsky's friend and senior, with whose benevolent support Tchaikovsky had taken his first steps. Then there had been Rachmaninov, whose trio "in memory of a great artist" had been dedicated in turn to Tchaikovsky. And now there was Shostakovich's Second Trio "In memory of I. I. Sollertinsky." Although dedicated to his friend, the trio—as always, with Shostakovich—went far beyond the composer's personal experience and private grief. Clearly, Shostakovich was not thinking of Sollertinsky alone when he wrote this work. He was probably remembering others who had died before their time, the tens and hundreds of thousands who had suffered at the hands of Hitler's forces at Auschwitz and Maidanek, Treblinka, and Buchenwald. The work evokes scenes of horrid phantasmagoria reminiscent of Picasso's *Guernica*; some passages throb with terror. Probably the most terrible and gloom-ridden of Shostakovich's works, the Second Trio is the only one in which there is neither relief nor reconciliation, where the forces of evil, destruction, and death prevail.

Shostakovich's mother, Sofia Vasilyevna

Dmitri in 1914

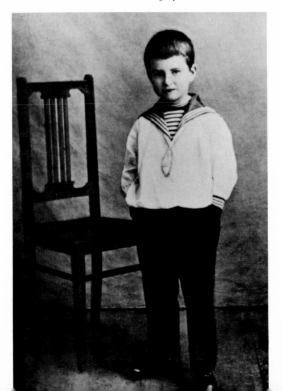

Dmitri with his sisters, Maria and Zoya, 1911

Shostakovich in 1923; with Ivan Sollertinsky in 1929; with
Vladimir Mayakovsky (center) and Vsevolod Meyerhold

Shostakovich and his first wife, Nina Vasilyevna, 1943; composition class
at the Moscow Conservatory, 1943; in the early 1940s

Shostakovich and his children, Maxim and Galya, at the family dacha in Komarova, 1948; with the poet Yevgeni Yevtushenko in the Great Hall of the Moscow Conservatory, 1962; with Benjamin Britten; with his son, Maxim, during rehearsals of the Fifteenth Symphony, 1972

[1944–1949]

In 1944 the entire Shostakovich family was reunited in Moscow. Before finally moving to the capital, the children had stayed in Kuibyshev in the care of Nina's parents. They lived apart until Nina had settled into the new apartment, furnishing it and providing it with everything needed. Now at last they were all together. Shostakovich had greatly missed the children. He loved them and their lively games and the hubbub they created.

Galya was almost nine years old and, to carry on the tradition established by Sofia, it was decided that she should begin to study music. It was for his daughter that the composer wrote the first of his teaching exercises, *Children's Notebook*, consisting of six pieces for piano. The pieces— *March, Waltz, The Bear, A Cheerful Tale, A Sad Tale*, and *The Clockwork Doll*—were written in order of difficulty for the beginner pianist. The first is the easiest—a march with a simple, clear-cut rhythm and an uncomplicated tune but that provides, with its sharp changes of dynamics and its varied ways of producing sound, interesting exercises for the young pianist. Then come further pieces of gradually increasing difficulty.

It was already the spring of 1945, and victory was near; the last volleys were thundering over Nazi Germany. Shostakovich's Eighth Symphony, representing a striving for peace, was being heard in the capitals of Europe liberated from Nazism, in performances by the world's best conductors. During the days of mourning when the American people were saying their farewells to President Roosevelt, Serge Koussevitzky gave a commemorative performance of the symphony's first movement, which left an indelible impression on the hearts of those who heard it.

The symphony was performed in its entirety in New York. An American critic wrote: "With his music Dmitri Shostakovich is doing more for the establishment of friendly relations between our country and Russia than any conferences or pacts could do. It is pointless to try to define genius: it is impossible to analyze the most significant of Shostakovich's work. It is not only interesting as sound, it also synthesizes all the musical elements with vital strength and expressiveness. The Eighth Symphony made me, as it were, experience with the composer the tragic and heroic episodes of the war years."

This magnificent music brought a warm and sympathetic response everywhere. By analogy with the Seventh Symphony, the *Leningrad*, it was sometimes referred to as the *Stalingrad*, recalling the heroic stand at the city on the Volga that changed the course of the war and ultimately assured the victory of the U.S.S.R.

By the time the Eighth Symphony was performed, Shostakovich was already thinking about his next symphonic cycle. His ideas in those memorable days were undoubtedly tied to the historic events then taking place. "What words, what musical ideas must be found to convey the feelings of Soviet man?" wrote the composer. "What strength and monumental artistic forms can convey the grandeur and courage of a warrior people? These images of a stern and glorious time crowd together in the mind of the artist, and we anticipate the joy of their creation, the painful joy of giving them shape in words, sounds, colors. I feel the epigraph to all our artistic work in the coming years will be the short yet portentous word "Victory."

Shostakovich conceived the idea of a new symphony—a Symphony of Victory. He had already begun to write the first movement and was seeking a literary text for the monumental choral conclusion. The work, however, remained only in the form of sketches. Asked why he did not finish the symphony, Shostakovich said many years later: "It didn't work out, nothing came of it." It was not within his capacities to compose such an epic, although there can be no doubt that the Soviet victory was for him, as for all Soviet people, a great joy.

In the first postwar months of 1945 Shostakovich worked on still another new symphony. Newspapers published reports of a première in preparation, and critics and music lovers waited to hear a monumental work written on the same scale as the two previous mighty symphonies, a work celebrating victory and the victors. The première of the Ninth Symphony on November 3, 1945—given in the Great Hall of the Leningrad Philharmonic under the direction of Yevgeni Mravinsky—somehow disappointed and surprised everyone. Lasting less than twenty-five minutes, it seemed a miniature work, brilliant, in some ways reminiscent of Prokofiev's *Classical Symphony* and having something in common with Mahler's Fourth. Outwardly unpretentious and classical in appearance, it clearly follows the principles of the Viennese symphonies of Haydn and Mozart.

The Ninth Symphony aroused the most contradictory opinions: some considered the new work "inopportune," while others thought the composer had "responded to the heroic victory of the Soviet people," that it was a "joyful sigh of relief." The symphony was defined as a "work of lyrical comedy, not without dramatic elements which accentuate the fundamental line of development," and as a "tragic-satirical pamphlet."

Which among these dissenting opinions and judgments should be given credence? Most authoritative, we believe, is the view expressed by the symphony's first interpreter, a conductor who was always sensitive and subtle in grasping the slightest nuance of Shostakovich's music. These are Mravinsky's words:

As a work directed against philistinism, I interpret the Ninth Symphony as an original "symphonic broadside" which ridicules complacency and bombast, the desire to "rest on one's laurels"—attributes and a state of mind which were particularly dangerous at a time when the war had just ended and the task of healing its wounds lay ahead. To be sure, not all the symphony is ironic—it contains both tender lyricism and deep sadness. The insouciant or frivolous "light-heartedness" of the first movement (think of the secondary subject!) and the element of deliberate and labored gaiety in the finale express, not the composer's own feelings, but those of his opposite—the self-satisfied, short-sighted philistine who is essentially indifferent to everything.

Calm, serene gaiety and the joyful play of sound were by no means characteristic of a composer who had been the artistic and civic conscience of his time. The Ninth Symphony, for all its brilliance, lightness, and perhaps even surface gloss, is by no means an unproblematic work. The joyful, open-hearted gaiety is interwoven in the music with the grotesque, the lyrical with the grief-stricken and the dramatic. There is a deliberate reference to the bitter irony of the Mahlerian "humoresque." In his Fourth Symphony Mahler, one of Shostakovich's favorite composers, departed for the first time from monumentalism and sharp dramatic conflicts to choose the lyrical and the grotesque as the basic forms with which to express his idea: the clash of the implied hero, the composer's "I," with a smug philistine world. Shostakovich's Ninth Symphony seems to be similar in content.

As usual the symphonic work was followed by compositions in other genres. Some of these were written in Moscow, others near Leningrad. Although Shostakovich had been living in Moscow since 1943, his heart was still in Leningrad. His native city was associated with all his memories of childhood and youth; here was where he had first known love, where the memory of his best friend remained, and where his people lived. His mother Sofia was still living in the small apartment on Dmitrov Lane with her eldest daughter and a nephew, and when he came to Leningrad Shostakovich always preferred her modest quarters to a hotel.

Numerous official duties brought him frequently to the city, apart from a natural desire to see his mother. In 1946 he was elected by his Leningrad colleagues as chairman of their Composers' Union. There was much to occupy him. The Union—newly housed in a beautiful old building designed by a famous St. Petersburg architect—had recently become very active. Shostakovich participated as chairman not only out of duty, but because of his intense interest in the future of Soviet music.

In 1947 Shostakovich became a deputy for Leningrad to the Supreme Soviet of the Russian Soviet Federal Socialist Republic. He was now spending a lot of time elsewhere than in the old residence on Herzen Street. As a deputy he held a reception once a month. He worked in premises especially allocated for the purpose, and an endless stream of people came to see him. Workers, civil servants, and pensioners, they came on business unrelated to music or to the composer's usual range of concerns, presenting their worries, needs, and complaints.

It was a difficult time: the country was only beginning to recover from the wounds of war. Shostakovich gave his assistance to the extent he could, patiently listening to those who came to see him and lending a sympathetic ear to the troubles of others. Then he would approach the various government departments, sending them petitions, applications, and official memoranda to help wounded veterans find interesting work within their capacities, to enable those whose houses had been destroyed by enemy bombs and shells to obtain accommodation, and to help those in need of medical treatment to enter a free sanatorium.

The composer always liked to take his vacations in the Leningrad area. From 1946 on he spent the summer months in the Karelian Isthmus northwest of the city, in picturesque places on the Gulf of Finland. Initially he rented a dacha in the village of Komarovo, or rather a house standing apart in the woods between the railway station and the Gulf, not far from the dacha settlement. Later, in the early 1950s, his father-in-law Vasili Varzar built his own two-story dacha in Komarovo as well.

In 1947 the composer attended the Prague Music Festival. On May 20 and 21 Mravinsky conducted the Eighth Symphony. He was fully aware of the responsibility he bore: performed six months previously in Prague, the work had been a total failure and had been subjected to severe criticism. The Soviet conductor's task was to "rehabilitate" one of Shostakovich's favorite works. Present at the concert were the President of the Republic, all the most prominent figures in Czech music, foreign guests, and representatives of the press. For Shostakovich this was his first appearance abroad at the performance of one of his works, and the first time that a foreign audience—foreign devotees of symphonic music and admirers of Soviet art—were able to see and welcome him.

The symphony met with tremendous success: the composer and conductor were not allowed to leave for a long time, the ovation lasting more than half an hour. The audience did not merely applaud—many shouted, banged their seats, or stamped their feet. Prague had not seen such a success, such a rapturous reception within living memory. The two concerts at which the Eighth was performed overshadowed all other events in the Prague Spring Festival. Soon after the concert Mravinsky received a letter: "The heroes of the Red Army and Soviet literature were already known to me," wrote one of those present at this historic concert. "But only now have I discovered what kind of heroes there are in Soviet music! I was familiar with the music of Tchaikovsky, Beethoven, Smetana, and others, but I had never heard such music as Shostakovich's Eighth Symphony. We had always liked the U.S.S.R. and assumed that our affection could not be deeper. Yet thanks to you and Shostakovich we find ourselves still more strongly attached to the Soviet Union. I greet you both with all my heart."

The composer returned to his country inspired. New ideas and new pupils awaited him, as did varied and onerous official duties. His time was scheduled not by days or even weeks, but by months. The class at the Conservatory increased in size, since many gifted musicians were anxious to study with him; film directors approached him with proposals; his Leningrad constituents looked forward to their deputy's reception day. Shostakovich loved this day-to-day ferment and could not bear to be unoccupied: this was the way he had been brought up since childhood.

The composer had a multitude of creative plans. It was an energetic period, active and crowded with events. Gathering together all its strength and mobilizing all its resources, the country was restoring itself, rising again from the ashes and ruins. The towns and villages devastated by the enemy, the scorched fields and forests, and the blown-up bridges, dams, and factories were being reborn. The entire people were gripped by an enthusiasm for work. Workers and peasants, engineers and scientists did not spare themselves in their efforts to heal the terrible wounds of war.

Those involved in art and culture did not stand idly by, and naturally Shostakovich shared in this general upsurge of activity. It was appropriate that in these years there appeared the suite for chorus and orchestra entitled *Leningrad, My Native City*, the *Poem on My Native Land*, and the music to the films *The Young Guard*, *Meeting on the Elbe*, and *The Fall of Berlin*, which told of the great struggle and victory of the Soviet people.

All this made what happened in early 1948 still more unexpected: Shostakovich and a number of other composers were subjected to severe criticism in the Soviet press. Shostakovich in no way wished to pose as an injured and unacknowledged genius. He could understand the grain of truth which lay behind the otherwise unfounded accusations: a people progressing toward mastery of all the wealth of culture, yet still only aspiring to its heights, needed art which was simpler in language and more accessible in form. At a meeting in Moscow of composers and musicologists, Shostakovich said that their common aim should be "work—persistent, creative, and joyful effort to produce new works which will find their way to the hearts of the Soviet people and which they will understand and love."

Shostakovich's works in this vein were the musical scores for the films *Vissarion Belinsky*, *The Unforgettable Year 1919*, and the oratorio *The Song of the Forests*. *The Song of the Forests*, an oratorio for soloists, boys' choir, mixed chorus, and symphony orchestra to verses by the Soviet poet Yevgeni Dolmatovsky, was written in 1949. The underlying concept of this work is the transition, through peaceful and constructive work, "from the past to the future," from the misfortunes and devastation of the recently ended war to the flowering of a happy life. The idea of the oratorio was not fortuitous, although the occasion of its composition seems to have been a chance conversation between the composer and the poet.

Dolmatovsky had visited the steppe near Stalingrad where large-scale construction and land-reclamation work was then in progress, and reported to Shostakovich about what he had seen. "He listened with remarkable attention. He had the gift of listening. The whole time ripples of animation passed across his face," Dolmatovsky recalled. "Then he said: 'You know, this is very poetic. It's very musical.'"

The composer was fascinated by the poetry involved in the creation of man-made forests. The next time he met Dolmatovsky he asked if the poet could write the words for an oratorio on the forests of the future, forests which would rustle where now there were only barren plains. The poet agreed. He showed his first drafts to Shostakovich and took the composer's observations into account. Only when work on the text had been completed did Shostakovich take it with him to Komarovo. He returned with the finished oratorio.

The première met with tremendous, triumphant success. The music captivated the audience by its brilliant craftsmanship, the clarity of its images, and its genuine optimism. Some musicians admittedly took the view that the work had been written to order and not from the heart—that it was a reply to criticism. Although indeed to some extent a "reply to criticism," it was a sincere reply from a man who never acted against his own conscience. The oratorio came into being because its theme corresponded to an inner need of the composer and was in harmony with his creative quest. As Dolmatovsky recalls, it was not for nothing that Shostakovich, meeting the poet by chance shortly before his death in 1975, said: "You know, *The Song of the Forests* was really about protecting the environment—a subject the whole world is talking about now. We hit the nail on the head!"

Of course this was not the only kind of music which occupied the composer. He lived in a world of sounds which mirrored all his feelings and thoughts. In them he poured out what perhaps he never said to anyone. All he had experienced he expressed in the First Violin Concerto—one of the best, most personal, and most tormented of Shostakovich's works, heard for the first time only in 1955.

Each of the concerto's movements has a title, or rather the genre of each is specified, indicating its content. The first, a nocturne, is conceived as a monologue for the violin with only a suggestion of orchestral accompaniment. The second, a scherzo, depicts cruel forces hostile to mankind and what is good—forces which bring suffering. In contrast to the scherzo, the third movement is a majestic and austere passacaglia. An enormous solo cadenza for the violin—yet another movement of the concerto—seems to be essentially a meditation. The finale, a burlesque, follows without a break and returns the listener to the whirl of everday life.

Throughout the concerto, either in concealed and cryptic form or clearly and distinctly, can be heard the composer's signature, made up of the notes DSCH—the first letters of his name and surname in German transliteration: D. Schostakowitsch. In this way the composer for the first time gave an account in music specifically of himself, of his own reflections and experiences, his own destiny.

In the same year, 1948, Shostakovich wrote a further work, the cycle *From Jewish Folk Poetry* for soprano, contralto, and tenor with piano accompaniment. Its origin was fortuitous: the composer had happened upon a collection of Jewish folklore at a newsstand. Thinking it contained the melodies of Jewish folk songs, Shostakovich asked to see the book. It had no music—only the poems were given, in Russian translation—but the texts made such a strong impression on the composer that he was at once inspired to write a song cycle.

From Jewish Folk Poetry does not consist of ballads or songs in the usual sense. The eleven numbers in the cycle are vivid dramatic miniatures of folk life. In this work, as in his operas, Shostakovich develops the tradition of Moussorgsky, to whom he felt akin. The composer creates apt graphic musical portraits of the cycle's dramatis personae, vivid sketches using the characteristic intonation of speech, its free and expressive rhythm and pungent harmonic coloring.

[1949–1955]

From 1949 on Shostakovich became still more actively involved in public affairs, and not merely within his own country. As a member of the Soviet Committee for the Defense of Peace he visited the United States for the meeting of the Cultural and Scientific Conference for World Peace. The solemn and stirring opening of the Conference took place on March 25 at the Waldorf-Astoria Hotel in New York. Scholars and prominent figures in culture and the arts were among the nearly three thousand delegates.

Shostakovich delivered a fervent address to the Conference in support of peace and democracy, making an impassioned appeal to artists all over the world:

> The forces we have at our disposal are truly limitless, for the overwhelming majority of mankind favors peace—all those who labor and create, without distinction of sex, age, religious convictions, or color.
>
> Our role—the role of the artistic intelligentsia: writers, artists, and musicians—is exceptionally important. We must raise our voices with all our strength in the cause of peace, truth, humanity, and the future of mankind. At this crucial stage in history we must not stand aloof consoling ourselves with empty illusions, as though we were outside life, above the struggle. No, we must enter into the very thick of life so that we may influence its course; we must keep pace with the progressive forces of mankind and take our place in the vanguard of those struggling for peace. In this struggle we

must participate with our art—with its content, ideas, images and its whole sense of direction.

It is extremely important that the energies of all progressive artists who support peace not be dissipated, that they strive together toward the common aim of serving the humane principles of peace, freedom, and democracy, sharing, developing, and using the valuable experience and achievements of a truly advanced art.

On the last day of the Conference Shostakovich played the scherzo from his Fifth Symphony in an arrangement for piano at an impressive rally in Madison Square Garden. Those present at the rally, about thirty thousand people, gave the Soviet composer a warm welcome.

This was his first visit to the United States. The Conference met for three days, with a crowded agenda of meetings, press conferences, receptions, and banquets. America interested Shostakovich, and he was anxious to see and hear more. He did succeed in setting aside a day to see New York, and managed to go to a Stokowski concert at Carnegie Hall and an evening recital by the Juilliard Quartet at Town Hall. Of course he had further plans to travel around the country and to give concerts in Washington, Boston, and New York. "We had done all we had to do and were looking forward to a pleasant vacation, and were hoping to get to know American life and culture," Shostakovich said later. "Instead, however, we received a message from the State Department delicately suggesting that we leave the country. We had to leave within three days. These three days we spent in Washington."

In 1950 Shostakovich visited Warsaw, where he took part in the Second World Peace Congress. Shostakovich was a member of the International Commission for Economic and Cultural Links. In one of his speeches he said: "True culture always serves peace, and a knowledge and a real understanding of the culture of any people reduce the danger of war. . . .

The more books written in different languages a person reads, the more symphonies he hears, the more paintings and films he sees, the clearer the great value of our culture will become to him, and the more criminal it will seem to him to destroy the culture or the life . . . of any person."

That same year saw the solemn observance in Leipzig of the bicentenary of the death of Johann Sebastian Bach. Many prominent musicians—composers, conductors, singers, and instrumentalists, as well as choral and orchestral ensembles —took part in the Bach Festival. In the course of this resplendent commemoration almost all of Bach's major works were performed.

Shostakovich also spent these days in the German Democratic Republic. He had been invited as an honorary guest, but found himself unexpectedly obliged to take part in the final concert of the Bach celebrations. The concert took place in the city's principal hall, the Friedrichstadtpalast. The finale of Shostakovich's First Symphony was among the works on the program, which was to conclude with Bach's Concerto in D Minor for Three Keyboards and Orchestra, to be played by the Soviet musicians Tatyana Nikolaeva, Maria Yudina, and Pavel Serebryakov. On the very eve of the concert, however, Yudina hurt her finger and was unable to appear, so without preparation Shostakovich agreed to take her place in the second piano part.

In the months that followed, the tremendous impression that the Bach Festival made on him evidently led Shostakovich to produce a new work, the Twenty-four Preludes and Fugues for Piano, written after the model of Bach's Well-Tempered Clavier. As with Bach, the preludes and fugues are written in all twenty-four keys, major and minor. Each fugue has a prelude which is inseparable from it, sometimes announcing the fugue's subject and sometimes setting it off by contrast. The composer's polyphonic technique is faultless and sharply defined. The music of the cycle is profoundly modern. The prevailing pattern is both gravely lyrical and pungently grotesque, epic power alternating with sorrowful folk melodies, the water-color translucency of landscape sketches being combined with unfaltering heroism, and the serenity of childhood with grave meditations.

By the early 1950s Shostakovich had written five string quartets. The Second, composed immediately after the funereal Trio, is dedicated to Shebalin. It is his only major work of the wartime years to contain no reflection of the tragic events of the war, and seems instead prevailingly bright, epic, and lyrical in its themes.

The Third String Quartet is dedicated to four magnificent musicians—Dmitri Tsyganov, Vasili Shirinsky, Vadim Borisovsky, and Sergei Shirinsky, the members of the Beethoven Quartet, an ensemble which even at that time was outstanding. Unlike its predecessor, the work is imbued with the echoes of the composer's experiences, although written more than a year after the war's end. Autobiographical elements can be traced in its five-movement structure, which recalls the Eighth Symphony. The "hero" of the quartet progresses from a serene childhood and the carefree and joyful discovery of life to an energetic and radiant second movement, then through the conflict and brutality of the third and the tragedy of the fourth to the enlightened maturity of the finale.

The Fourth Quartet, written in 1949, resembles the Third in its mood and musical language. The Fifth, however, also dedicated to the Beethoven Quartet, is composed in a quite different mold. Here the musical conflict is defined in terms of the clash of two diametrically opposed motifs—one brutal and aggressive, the other fragile, pure, and lyrical. While the preceding works in quartet form were associated with the Eighth Symphony and the First Violin Concerto, this quartet, written in 1952, anticipates the Tenth Symphony, which Shostakovich composed the following year.

He wrote the symphony during the summer at the dacha in Komarovo, where as in all recent years he spent his vacation. He would come from Moscow with the children. Sometimes Nina would accompany them but more often she was not present, having gone instead to Armenia, where groups of physicists were doing research on cosmic rays. But Shostakovich's mother Sofia would come from Leningrad, and sometimes they were joined by his sister Maria with her grown-up son and her grandson.

This big, noisy family spent the time enjoyably. The children looked for mushrooms, ran to the shore of the Gulf to bathe, and cycled. They were accompanied by the dogs which were always part of the Shostakovich household. Often Shostakovich too would take part in their simple but never boring pastimes. He would take a bicycle and go to the woods, cycling unhurriedly along the forest paths, methodically indicating turns by signaling with his arm.

He was very fond of Komarovo: he always felt comfortable there and never complained of the cold, damp weather which often descended. It suited him much better than the heat and burning sun of the South, and his work was always remarkably fruitful at the dacha. As a rule, these summer months were the most productive. When the music which had already been created in his mind, thought out, and experienced, made itself consciously felt, the composer sat down at his writing table.

He was now working almost continuously: he rose early in the morning and immediately set to work on his manuscript. He left his writing table only for breakfast, lunch, and dinner, and afterward would hurry back to his manuscript and his music. His method of working was distinctive. First of all he would set out a synopsis of the movement—the major themes, their combination and development, with an indication of the tone coloring. From this synopsis he would later write the score straight onto the page without corrections.

From the end of July through September 1953 he was composing the Tenth Symphony, which emerged as one of Shostakovich's most important works. "Few contemporary composers could have reflected the griefs and hopes of contemporary man as Shostakovich has in his Tenth Symphony," wrote his Czech colleague Václav Dobiaš. The symphony was given its première in Leningrad at the end of the year; Mravinsky, as was the tradition, conducted.

The first performance evoked a multitude of conflicting judgments and contradictory opinions. From force of habit many still thought in terms of the recent past, reproaching the composer for the complexity of his musical language, for according too little prominence to the underlying heroic and optimistic features of the work, and for its predominantly somber tone. But a different point of view prevailed. "I am deeply convinced that the conflict it portrays arises from the tension now existing throughout the world," wrote Dmitri Kabalevsky of the Tenth Symphony. Said David Oistrakh: "The Symphony is imbued with the lofty ethical principles, deep humanity, and genuine feeling of a great artist and patriot. Its strength lies in its enormous dramatic effect, its sharp conflicts, and the captivating beauty and propriety of its language." Soon the symphony was also accorded recognition abroad.

That same year, 1953, Shostakovich wrote a further work, the Concertino for Two Pianos, which he composed for his son. The fifteen-year-old Maxim, a student at the music school attached to the Moscow Conservatory, played it at one of the regular concerts with a fellow student, Alla Maloletkova. The concertino surprised listeners accustomed to Shostakovich's stern and dramatic muse. Although technically not very difficult, it was effective and seemed to be a distinctly virtuoso work. Its music is distinguished by youthful ardor and directness of feeling, slyness, exuberance, and mischievousness. A composer who had felt and lived through so much seemed to have rediscovered his youth.

Shostakovich's next composition was also full of joy, sunlight, and limitless energy. This is the effervescent *Festive Overture*, written in 1954, which seems to pour out in one breath. Even now, almost twenty-five years later, it impresses the listener as a truly spirited, heartening, and attractive work.

Less than a month after the première of the *Festive Overture*, grief settled on the Shostakovich household for a prolonged period. Nina had as usual been spending a lot of time traveling between her permanent post in Moscow and the physics research center in Armenia. She was expected home in early December. Her ticket had been bought and a telegram had arrived asking them to meet her at the station. But within two days a second and most alarming telegram arrived. Nina had felt unwell on the train. She was taken with a suspected volvulus to Yerevan, where an operation was performed immediately. Nothing, however, could be done to help. Within three days—the first three days of December—Nina, still young and full of the joy and strength of life, had died. Shostakovich took the first flight to Yerevan when he received the alarming telegram, but was in time only to bid her farewell. A few days later the coffin was transported to Moscow. The funeral took place on a cold, bleak, gloomy day. The music of the Eighth Symphony was played at the graveside.

The year 1955 brought two major musical events, but also a second enormous loss.

The cycle *From Jewish Folk Poetry* was performed in January in the Small Hall of the Philharmonic, the elegant concert hall where music had been played for two hundred years and where the St. Petersburg public had rapturously welcomed Franz Liszt and Clara Schumann. The singers taking part—Nina Dorliak, Zara Dolukhanova, and Aleksei Maslennikov—were superb, and the composer himself played the piano part. The work was a triumphant success, but for Shostakovich the occasion was clouded by the grave condition of his mother, who was dying. She was growing thin and weak and could scarcely eat.

In the summer, living as usual in the dacha at Komarovo, Shostakovich did not seclude himself in his study. He tried to spend as much time as he could with his mother and talked to her a great deal, looking after her with touching care. In the fall he returned to Moscow. The children were beginning a new school year, while for him this was the start of a new musical season. As always he had many duties to attend to in the Composers' Union and other official organizations.

Shosktakovich was very busy at the Conservatory, and not only when teaching composition. Genuinely interested in the proper education of young musicians as composers, performers, and musicologists, he went to student concerts, meetings of the students' academic association, and sessions of the Youth Section of the Composers' Union, to which the student composers belonged.

In October Shostakovich again arrived in Leningrad to prepare for the première of his Violin Concerto, having waited seven years for its first performance. Yevgeni Mravinsky conducted and David Oistrakh was the violin soloist. The première was given on October 29 and 30.

By early November Shostakovich had already gone to Austria to take part in the celebrations honoring the reopening of the Vienna Opera House, which had been destroyed during World War II. In Vienna, on November 9, he received word that his mother had died. He managed to fly to Leningrad to accompany her on her last journey. The funeral took place on November 12, his sister Maria's birthday. It was dank and windy—a typical autumn day for Leningrad. From the Novovolkovsk cemetery they returned to the apartment on Dmitrov Lane where his mother had lived for twenty-two years. Following the old Russian custom, they sat down at the table to remember the deceased. Shostakovich was deeply saddened and silent. A witness at this sorrowful gathering could recall him saying only, "How cold and alone she is now."

[1955–1960]

Everything in life is intermingled—joy and grief, success and failure, ascent and decline. The mid-1950s were associated with major changes in the country. The Communist Party resolutely revealed the mistakes which had been committed as a result of the cult of personality, and Lenin's standards were restored. A fresh wind of change was blowing everywhere and the composer, who since childhood had reacted keenly to everything around him, could not but respond in his music and in all his activities to the historic changes.

Shostakovich made fervent pronouncements in the press, at plenary sessions and meetings of the Composers' Union, concerned as he was for the fortunes of Soviet music. In the days preceding the opening of the Second Congress of Soviet Composers, he published an article devoted to the most pressing questions of the day.

> Every discovery of the new in art is attended by some degree of experiment, and the bolder, the more wide-ranging, the more individual the artist's concept, the more his experimentalism will be apparent and the more he "risks." Even as he overcomes the difficulties which arise, the artist will experience partial failures, failures which appear as such only at first glance. Yet this is not so bad, provided the artist's general ideological and aesthetic tendency is sound and directed toward the truth of life.
>
> Some proponents of hasty and dogmatic formulae, however, have no regard for the complexity and many-sidedness of the subject under discussion. To them, the very intention

of understanding something in depth seems at times suspicious—an activity emanating "from the devil." In this way trivial and primitive definitions arise, sometimes offered in the name of Marxist-Leninist aesthetics, which in fact discredit the dialectically flexible and subtle methods of the Marxist-Leninist analysis of art.

We must develop and encourage a diversity of approach in our thinking about music; in this field, what is required is a daring spirit of innovation.

The attitude of critics toward his work had changed conspicuously. No one now had any doubt about the enormous value of Shostakovich's compositions, and there was an increasing number of serious articles devoted to his music, whether to general aspects or particular works.

Throughout these years Shostakovich continued to appear in concerts as a pianist. Not for a long time, admittedly—not since 1930—had he played anyone else's music except on rare occasions: he had no time to work on programs or to keep himself in proper pianistic trim. But he played his own compositions regularly: the Quintet, the Trio, the Sonata for Cello and Piano, some of the Preludes and Fugues, and the First Piano Concerto.

In a book on his teacher, Samari Savshinsky—also a pupil of Nikolaev and himself one of the most important piano teachers in Leningrad—described Shostakovich as a pianist:

> He is an outstanding artist and performer. The crystalline clarity and precision of thought, the almost ascetic absence of embellishment, the precise rhythm, technical perfection, and very personal timbre he produced at the piano all made Shostakovich's piano playing individual in the highest degree, and made him an irreplaceable interpreter of such works as the Quintet and the best of his Preludes. Those who remember Shostakovich's performance of Beethoven's

mighty *Hammerklavier* Sonata, followed by a number of Chopin pieces, can only regret that his talent as a pianist was never fully developed or applied.

During the 1950s Shostakovich played in cities as far apart as Moscow and Minsk, Vilnius and Yerevan, Kaunas and Baku, Riga and Kishinev, but he appeared most frequently in his beloved Leningrad. There, in the Great Hall of the Philharmonic, a concert of his music—the Fifth Symphony, the cantata *Poem of Our Fatherland*, and the First Piano Concerto—was given on May 19, 1956. Shostakovich was very nervous at the rehearsals, so rarely did he appear as a soloist. He paused frequently, asking for one difficult passage or another to be repeated. The concert went off successfully, but after it had ended he announced: "Today was my last appearance as a pianist—such performances are very taxing for me. I haven't practiced regularly at the piano for many years, and when I have to perform I get very nervous!"

Despite this decision Shostakovich did give several more performances, including appearances abroad at the Salle Chaillot in Paris, where he played the First and Second Piano Concertos. But these were his last performances as a soloist. From the end of the 1950s on, he took part in concerts of his works only as an accompanist to singers or as a member of an instrumental ensemble.

Events in the second half of the 1950s brought the composer new strength. Shostakovich was returning to the themes which had preoccupied his thoughts at the outset of his career. It was now time, he felt, to give form to those ideas which had not been realized: the people, the Revolution, Lenin.

Shostakovich had taken up these themes on several occasions. He had written the symphonies dedicated to the First of May and to the October Revolution. Later had come plans for a symphony dedicated to Lenin. In 1951, when the experiences of the war had already receded, he returned to the subject of the Revolution by writing ten choral pieces: *Courage, My Friends, We Are Advancing!, One of Many, To the Streets!, An Encounter During an Exchange of Letters, To the Executed, The Ninth of January, At Last the Guns Fell Silent, They Conquered, May Song*, and *Song*. These were austere, stirring choruses inspired by old revolutionary songs.

Then in 1957, on the fortieth anniversary of Soviet rule, appeared the Eleventh Symphony with the programmatic title *The Year 1905* (1905 was the year of the first Russian Revolution). It had begun tragically when, on the frosty Sunday afternoon of January 9, masses of working people moved from the outskirts of St. Petersburg toward the Winter Palace. This was no anti-government demonstration—quite the opposite: the workers went with their wives and children to the Tsar as to a protector and patron, carrying icons and banners.

"Bloody Sunday found me in the streets," recalled Alexandra Kollontai, one of the most outstanding women of the Revolution, who subsequently became a prominent Soviet diplomat and spent many years in Sweden as ambassador of the U.S.S.R.

> I went with the demonstrators to the Winter Palace, and the spectacle of the savage violence meted out to unarmed working people imprinted itself forever on my memory.
>
> January 9 was sunny and frosty. From every corner of St. Petersburg the city's poor wound their way in endless files toward the Tsar's palace. The lines of demonstrators criss-crossed the old city like the threads of a spider web. The people crowded close to the palace and waited. They waited patiently for an hour, then another hour: would the Tsar not come out to them? Who would accept the petition—the workers' petition to the Tsar?

But the Tsar did not emerge. The entreaties of the unarmed people were answered by a bugle call. It rang out with
unusual resonance and clarity in the frosty air. We could not
help glancing at one another.

"What's that?" someone beside me asked.

"It's the signal for the troops to straighten ranks," said
someone in the crowd reassuringly.

Again we waited, tense and with a vague foreboding. Another signal. The troops stirred slightly. Yet the crowd was
still smiling. It was an unarmed crowd which waited and
hoped, shifting from foot to foot from the cold and the frost.
There was a third signal, and then an unusual booming sound. What's that? They're shooting? "It's nothing,"
said a voice, "those are just blanks." Yet people were fall-
ing nearby—women, children—the children dropping like
wounded sparrows in the snow from the railings of the
Alexandrovsk Gardens. "Don't worry, it's an accident." The
people could not believe what was happening. But the Tsar's
mounted police were already galloping to the attack—to
attack the people!

The Tsar's crime against his own people raised a storm of
indignation: the Revolution had begun.

These were the events to which Shostakovich decided to
give musical substance. The result was a monumental symphony, his Eleventh. It has four movements without a break,
as if each flowed from its predecessor. Each movement has a
programmatic title.

The first is called *Palace Square*. This portrait in sound
makes a powerful impression. Here is the moribund, airless,
bureaucratic city of the Tsars. Yet it is also a generalization:
this inspired music evokes not merely the Palace Square of
the title, or St. Petersburg, but the whole vast country of
Russia, where freedom is stifled, life and thought suppressed,
and human dignity trampled underfoot.

The title of the second movement is *The Ninth of January*;

the music depicts the people's procession, the supplications and anguish of the unfortunate, and the appalling carnage that took place on the Tsar's orders. The third movement, *Eternal Memory*, is a requiem for those who perished, and the finale, *The Tocsin*, portrays the people's anger and their rebellion.

From a purely musical point of view, the remarkable feature of the Eleventh Symphony is that the composer created almost none of its themes, taking them instead from revolutionary and prison songs; very probably it is these which give the work its visual immediacy. Yet they are by no means merely quotations, nor are they extraneous elements incorporated into the symphony. They live, breathe, and develop in symphonic terms in the same way as any of the composer's themes. They become an organic part of Shostakovich's music.

The Eleventh Symphony was heard in Moscow and Leningrad at almost the same time. Nathan Rakhlin conducted the première in Moscow and Yevgeni Mravinsky the one in Leningrad. The critics greeted the work with unusually unanimous acclaim: "Not for a long time, not since Moussorgsky, has Russian art produced such an immensely powerful musical tragedy which has its source in the people."

The symphony was heard abroad within the year. "Shostakovich . . . has reached the heights. . . . The symphony shows its creator's mastery as well as the strength and richness of his artistic personality, which has achieved its summation"—such were the comments of the Paris newspapers after the performance of the Eleventh Symphony at the Salle Chaillot. "Such music really could not fail to move any audience." "The Symphony is a monumental fresco, at once a film in music and a revolutionary song, an epic and a surging affirmation of faith. We hear the rattle of machine-guns, the thunder of artillery, the voices of the crowd marching and singing, crying out under fire, and then lamenting the fallen."

In 1958 Shostakovich received the country's highest award —the Lenin Prize—for the Eleventh Symphony. The same year he visited many foreign countries to receive other important awards and distinctions, becoming a Commander of the French Order of Arts and Letters, a member of the British Royal Academy of Music, and an Honorary Doctor of Music of Oxford University. And at a ceremony in Helsinki he was awarded the International Jan Sibelius Prize.

After his mother's death, which had followed so soon after the death of his wife Nina, the composer felt alone and abandoned. His loneliness was intensified by the fact that his children had grown up. Galina, already twenty, had long been independent and had definitely chosen biology for her profession. Maxim, who was eighteen, remained faithful to music: he entered the Pianoforte Faculty of the Conservatory and dreamed of becoming a conductor, but had his own interests, too—his circle of friends and contemporaries. For the time being the two children lived with their father, but Shostakovich knew that this would not be for long: both would soon have their own families and be launched upon their own lives, entirely separate from his. For one who had never been alone, and who since early childhood had always been surrounded by those dear to him, the emptiness now gaping around him was unendurable. In 1959, however, a new and profound feeling entered his life.

In the previous year, 1958, Shostakovich had written an operetta entitled *Moscow, Cheryomushky*. Its subject was the comic adventures of people who had recently settled in Moscow. At that time there was a large number of such new residents. Building in the capital was expanding at a frenzied pace, so that every day people were moving into new blocks and apartments, as housing districts sprang up in the older suburbs. One of these, Cheryomushky, was particularly well known, and residents of other cities often used this name to describe their own new housing districts. "This is our Cheryomushky," those living in Gorky or Leningrad, Kursk or Oryol could be heard to say.

When the Mayakovsky Operetta Theater, anxious to extend its repertoire, asked some of the leading Soviet composers to write a work for it, Shostakovich complied.* The appearance of such a work was completely unexpected. Shostakovich was normally thought of as a symphonic composer, the author of philosophical and tragic works. Perhaps he was remembering his youth: the vivid satirical music to *The Bedbug*, written by Mayakovsky and produced by Meyerhold; the brilliant parodies of film music; and the mischievous passages in his ballets. Both at that time and later in the postwar years the composer had also written wonderful songs with beautiful, memorable tunes going straight to the heart. The first of these, *Song about a Passer-by*, composed to verses by Boris Kornilov, was written in 1932 for the film *The Passer-by*, directed by S. Yutkevich and F. Ermler. The song, beginning with the words "Cool morning greets us," is lively and tuneful, and gained instant popularity both in the Soviet Union and abroad. Subsequently, with different words, it became the anthem of the United Nations. All these elements were revived in the operetta *Moscow, Cheryomushky*, and a quotation from the *Song about a Passer-by* could even be heard in an aria sung by one of the heroines.

After the operetta had been produced in the theater, the

* Apart from Shostakovich's operetta, it was at about this period that Dmitri Kabalevsky's *Song of Spring* and Tikhon Khrennikov's *One Hundred Devils and a Girl* were written for the same theater.

Soviet Composer Publishing House undertook publication of a vocal score. Besides the editor who read the proofs of the score, a literary editor, Irina Antonovna Supinskaya, began work on the operetta. The young woman made a great impression on Shostakovich. Her intelligence and subtle taste were out of the ordinary, as were her penetrating and far-reaching opinions. She was very reserved and conscientious, but she had sensitivity, tact, and feminine charm. Despite her youth she gave the impression of being a person who had experienced a great deal.

The impression was not misleading. Irina had been born into a family belonging to the old St. Petersburg intelligentsia. Her father was an important linguistics scholar and ethnographer who worked for the Russian Museum, while her mother was a teacher. When still very young she lost her parents. The little girl stayed in the care of her grandparents, who tried as best they could to take the place of her mother and father. In 1941 they remained in Leningrad and endured all the horrors of the siege. It was not until the early spring of 1942 that the family was brought out by the "road of life." The path across the ice of Lake Ladoga—the only link between the besieged city and the rest of the country—was extremely hazardous. Day and night Nazi aircraft bombed the narrow strip along which continuous streams of vehicles wound their way into Leningrad delivering supplies and medicines, and out of the city carrying children, old people, the sick, and those who could not help in the defense. Over the lake at night wreaths of flares burned with a deathly light like fantastic chandeliers, while on both sides of the track, where the ice had been smashed by bombs and shells, crippled vehicles lay strewn about. A car brought the seven-year-old Irina and her grandparents to Kobona, a small station on the east bank of Lake Ladoga where the railway began. Already the worst seemed behind them but on the way, as the train moved through shells and bombs toward Moscow, both the old people died from the hardships they had undergone, leaving the little girl entirely alone. It is difficult to imagine how she reached Kuibyshev—the very city where Shostakovich lived during the evacuation—to find her only relative, an aunt on her mother's side.

In 1943 Irina and her aunt had gone to Moscow, and from that time on she lived in the capital. She graduated from a teacher's training institute, studied language and literature, and in 1955 joined the Soviet Composer Publishing House.

That year Shostakovich's creative plans involved a Concerto for Cello and Orchestra and an orchestral edition of Moussorgsky's opera *Khovanshchina*. Initially there was no question of his tackling the whole opera. The film director Vera Stroeva had had the idea of making a film based on Moussorgsky's opera and turned to Shostakovich for assistance. He was asked to edit the work and, if necessary, orchestrate those scenes to appear in the film. The composer, who greatly admired Moussorgsky, was delighted to accept. His participation in the film was not confined to the original assignment: he became co-author with the scriptwriter A. Abramova and, becoming enamored of the work, orchestrated not only the material needed for the film but the whole opera. This enormous task was carried out in an unprecedentedly short space of time. Shostakovich pored over the score for weeks, literally without respite, tearing himself away only for the most pressing concerns. Toward the end of the score he began to feel a pain in his right hand, so for a while he stopped working.

Then, after an interval of exactly ten years, he visited the West for the second time, to become a member of the American Academy of Sciences and an honorary professor of the

Mexican Conservatory. This time he had the opportunity to get to know the United States. On his return he gave his children an enthusiastic account of the trip, especially of Disneyland, where he sampled all the attractions. From his early years he had retained a genuine and childlike love for such things. A long time before, in his youth, Sollertinsky and he had been in the habit of going to the park at the People's Center. The two friends had taken great delight in the roller-coaster, which was known as the "American Hills." (Why this much-loved attraction was so called remains a mystery—in other Soviet cities it was known as the "Russian Hills"!) In September 1932 it was destroyed in a fire, greatly to the distress of Shostakovich and Sollertinsky. Now, more than a quarter of a century later and on the other side of the world, the composer must have found himself remembering his youth. Yet it is unlikely that his children listened to their father's stories with due attention, for both were already grown and such diversions no longer interested them; Galina had recently married, and Maxim's wedding was not far off.

That winter, anticipating that his family would expand in the near future, the composer bought a comfortable and spacious two-story house in Zhukovka, not far from Moscow. For the most part, however, he lived at the dacha, and as always he did a great deal of work. His hand, however, was still painful, and in February 1960 he had to go into a hospital. By the time he came out he had recovered, and feeling able now to write down what he composed, he returned once more to his work.

The outcome was the Seventh Quartet, dedicated to the memory of his wife Nina. The work was given its première in the Small Hall of the Leningrad Philharmonic. There is no grief in the Quartet, for almost five years had elapsed since Nina's death, and the bitterness of loss had softened. What remained were unclouded memories, regret, and sadness. Obviously this was a leave-taking: Shostakovich was bidding farewell to one who had shared his life for more than twenty years, who had been his friend and the mother of his children.

[1960–1963]

Three further works appeared in 1960. He composed the Satires to verses by the early twentieth-century Russian poet Sasha Chorny—a continuation of those parodistic works of his youth which Shostakovich had undoubtedly recalled when writing his recent operetta. He also wrote music for a Soviet–East German film called *Five Days, Five Nights*, dealing with the events of the last war. He worked on this score in Dresden, where he spent the summer months. The beautiful city of Dresden had been swept off the face of the earth in a single night, but was now rising again from the ruins, all of which stirred old feelings seemingly locked in his past. It is not without cause that he dedicated the Eighth Quartet, composed at the same time as the music for the film, to the memory of the victims of Nazism and war.

Written in no more than three days, as if poured from the depths of the artist's soul, the quartet is autobiographical. The composer is telling us about himself, but not merely in the same way as in, for example, the Tenth Symphony, in which his musical signature is heard. In the course of the quartet's five continuous movements, themes from various compositions make their appearance—from the opening subject of the First Symphony, which is interwoven with the largo of the first movement, to motifs from the movement entitled *Eternal Memory* in the Eleventh Symphony.

As always, the first performance of the quartet took place

in Leningrad on October 2, but Shostakovich was unable to attend. Maxim had married in September, and at the height of the wedding festivities his father had stumbled and broken his leg. Once again he went to the hospital, where he spent long, painful days unable to move. Of course he continued to work—he always worked. Naturally he viewed this as an absurd mischance and assumed that everything would clear up completely. But what had in fact set in was a serious and implacable disease of the central nervous system which poisoned the last fifteen years of his life. The first indication had appeared a year before, after *Khovanshchina*; this was the second.

On leaving the hospital, Shostakovich lived largely in Zhukovka. From there he traveled to his work at the Conservatory, and to conferences and meetings of artists at the Composers' Union. From 1960 on he was First Secretary of the board of the Composers' Union of the Russian Federation, a post whose duties he fulfilled punctually and conscientiously. The following year brought another honorary public duty: work on the Committee awarding the Lenin and State Prizes for literature and art. Although intermittent, this duty entailed no small outlay of time once a year, when the competing compositions were considered. Shostakovich would put aside all other concerns, devoting days or even weeks to acquainting himself with the new works.

Some years before, when the Eleventh Symphony was being rehearsed in concert halls, its sequel had begun to take shape in the composer's thoughts: the second movement of a symphonic dialogue on a revolutionary and historical theme —a symphony evoking the unforgettable days of October 1917. The Revolution was once again at the center of Shostakovich's attention, and once again he intended to paint a musical portrait of his native city, St. Petersburg/Petrograd. But this time the composer finally decided to carry out a scheme first envisaged decades before: to create a monumental canvas dedicated to Vladimir Ilyich Lenin.

Shostakovich had this to say about his new Twelfth Symphony:

> The symphony will have four movements. I saw the first as a musical account of Lenin's arrival in Petrograd in April 1917 and his meeting with the workers, the working class of Petrograd. The second movement depicts the historic events of November 7. The third will portray the Civil War, and the fourth the victory of the Great October Socialist Revolution. . . .
>
> It is difficult to talk about one's own compositions, but I am very excited by the theme of the new symphony, and it seems that this work will become a significant landmark in my artistic career. I attach great importance to it.
>
> Where am I turning for help in carrying out this project? Many things have certainly influenced the creation of my Twelfth Symphony: literature, the cinema, Soviet painting, and poetry. But what has served as my main creative impulse has been the fact that, although I was very young at the time, I was an eyewitness of the Great October Socialist Revolution. I was living in Petrograd at the time, and the events of that period have remained in my memory all my life.

Later, when the music was being written, the composer's plan underwent certain changes. The arrangement of the movements turned out differently: the musical portrayal of the Civil War was dropped, and in its place appeared a philosophically sublime adagio expressing the ideas of Lenin.

The Twelfth Symphony is a heroic epic, the portrait of a suffering, struggling, and conquering people. Its four movements have programmatic subtitles. The first, *Revolutionary Petrograd*, gives a general picture of the revolutionary city and conveys a sense of historic events to come.

The second, *The Flood*, is at the same time a landscape in music and a profound meditation. In Russian—*Razliv*—it is also the name of a lake to the north of Petrograd, on one of whose small islands Lenin hid from the police of the Provisional Government on the eve of the October Revolution. The music conveys both the feelings evoked by the restrained northern landscape and thoughts about the great leader.

The third movement is specifically devoted to the events of that October night remembered throughout the world. It is called *The Aurora* in honor of the legendary cruiser which, by firing a blank charge from one of its guns, gave the signal for the start of revolutionary activity. A distinct, almost visible picture emerges: an autumn night with swiftly flowing water; then, like a still from a film, the dark bulk of the vessel which was to become a symbol of the Revolution takes shape before the spectator-listener. Then the symphony's finale, *The Dawn of Humanity*, gives a panoramic view of the Revolution, celebrating its jubilant victory.

Shostakovich finished the Twelfth Symphony in 1961. On October 1, 1961, the opening day of the Twentieth Congress of the Communist Party of the Soviet Union, it was first heard simultaneously in the Great Hall of the Leningrad Philharmonic, conducted as always by Mravinsky, and in the city of Kuibyshev, still remembered by the composer from the sad days of war, evacuation, anxiety, and deprivation.

At the end of the same year, on December 30, Shostakovich's Fourth Symphony was given its première in Moscow. The symphony had waited a quarter of a century for this first performance and had all but perished amid the vicissitudes of its complex fate. When the composer had canceled the première during the orchestral rehearsals in the fall of 1936, his own manuscript was the only copy of the score. This was lost during the war, and he had come to the bitter conclusion that the work had perished. The orchestral parts, however, had been preserved by the Leningrad Philharmonic, and its librarian, Boris Shalman, had re-created the score from the parts—an enormous and painstaking task. In addition there existed an arrangement for two pianos which had been made by Levon Atovmyan, one of Shostakovich's friends.

At its première the symphony enjoyed tremendous success. The audience was astonished by its grandeur and power. The critics wrote:

> The piece is an extremely abrupt and graphic juxtaposition of nobility and frighteningly iconoclastic grotesquerie, the courage and beauty of creation and destructive skepticism, and the cruel struggle between the *human* and the blind and mechanically *inhuman* which stands opposed to it.
>
> . . . It seems that here we have reached a frontier in the expression of grief, personal suffering, and the illusoriness of dreams; after this, art either comes to an end or turns toward "the light, joy, a kind of 'convalescence' after a serious 'crisis.' "

For the composer the year 1961 was notable for a further important event: his return to his alma mater, the Leningrad Conservatory. Professor Orest Yevlakhov, who headed the composition faculty in Leningrad, asked Shostakovich to give postgraduate classes. Although well aware how much this would complicate his life, overburdened as he was with obligations, Shostakovich nonetheless agreed. He still loved his native city and the Conservatory where he had studied. It was arranged that he should take a postgraduate class twice a month. Some young composers who had just graduated from the Conservatory became his pupils, among them Boris Tishchenko, Gennadi Belov, and Vladislav Uspensky.

So once again Shostakovich found himself, as in the old days before the war, going to Room 36 on the second floor, at the corner of the long corridor—the room named after the Conservatory's earliest and most famous teacher, Rimsky-

Korsakov, where the composition class was traditionally held. Once again the young Leningrad students listened attentively to their favorite composer and mentor. All their lives they would recall their meetings with him, meetings which were emotionally and intellectually most stimulating.

The composer lived less and less in Moscow, spending his time increasingly in travel. In Moscow life was taking its own course. His children's families were growing up and having children of their own. Galya's son Andryusha was in his second year, and Maxim's first child had been born and was named Dmitri Shostakovich, perpetuating the composer's name and line.

In 1962 Shostakovich married Irina Supinskaya. She was a faithful and self-sacrificing friend in the last thirteen years of his life. He was no longer alone.

There were other reasons, too, why this year was to become noteworthy in Shostakovich's life. His favorite opera, which had caused him so much suffering, was revived. Once again the opera houses of Moscow and Leningrad heard *Katerina Izmailova*. This was the title by which the work became known in its new edition, replacing its previous title, *Lady Macbeth of Mtsensk District*; the new title was in fact a reversion to the original one used in the Nemirovich-Danchenko production thirty years before. This change was appropriate: the ironic reference in Leskov's tale was not wholly apposite to Shostakovich's work, in which the heroine is seen rather as a victim of the social structure than as predestined to wickedness. The première took place in the Maly Theater of the Leningrad Opera.

A few days earlier Shostakovich's latest symphony, the Thirteenth, composed to poems by the young poet Yevgeni Yevtushenko, had been performed in Moscow. This was Shostakovich's first encounter with Yevtushenko, and it

marked the beginning of their artistic and personal friendship. Said Shostakovich:

> Initially I wrote a sort of vocal and symphonic poem to
> Yevgeni Yevtushenko's poem "Babi Yar." Then I thought of
> continuing the work by setting other verses by the same poet.
> For the second movement I chose the poem "Humor," and
> for the third "In the Shop." The poem "Fears," which
> forms the basis of the fourth movement, was written by
> Yevtushenko with my symphony specifically in mind. For
> the finale I selected "A Career." There is no thread linking
> the subject matter of these poems. They were published at
> different times and are concerned with different themes, but
> I wanted to give them a musical unity. I was writing a sym-
> phony, not a series of individual musical tableaux. Those I've
> shown the work to say that I succeeded in what I set out
> to do.

The idea of the symphony came to him in the spring of
1961, but work on it could not begin immediately. The music
germinated in his thoughts, its outlines becoming increasingly
distinct. Unfortunately, the writing of the orchestral score had
to be done in the hospital, as had occurred before and would
later become the rule.

Shostakovich spent a month in the hospital, from June 20
to July 20, 1962. From there he wrote to one of his oldest
and closest friends, Vissarion Shebalin:

Moscow, July 1, 1962.

Dear Ronya,

I was extremely glad to get a letter from you. I couldn't
reply at once because there was a slight deterioration in my
right hand and I was forbidden to write for a while. Now
my hand has improved and I can write. At the moment I'm
in the hospital. I'll be spending another two weeks or so

here. They're treating my hand, so far not very successfully. . . .

In the hospital I began composing a Thirteenth Symphony. More accurately, it'll be a symphonic suite with voices
in five movements. The elements involved are a bass soloist,
bass chorus, and a symphony orchestra. I've used texts by
the poet Yevgeni Yevtushenko. Closer acquaintance with this
poet has made it clear to me that he's a major and, most important, a thoughtful talent. I've gotten to know him and like
him a lot. He's 29 [sic!]. It's very gratifying that young people like him are appearing among us.

The symphony has five movements. The first three are
completely finished. The fourth and fifth are making progress, less so in the case of the fourth. Yevtushenko has not
yet finished "Fears." A book of his poems has just come
out. If you come across it, read it.

By the time he left the hospital, the composer had all but
finished the symphony. This was in August, when he took a
vacation in the small town of Solotcha near Ryazan. Of his
latest work he said: "The social conduct of the individual as
a citizen has always interested me, and that's what was on
my mind. In the Thirteenth Symphony I set forth the problem of civic responsibility."

In this symphony the composer took a further step forward in giving specific form to his musical ideas. After the
"pure" symphonic structures of the Eighth, Ninth, and Tenth
Symphonies, and the programmatic Eleventh and Twelfth
with their subtitles, he had arrived at vocal and instrumental
forms linked to the word, to texts in verse. The central idea
of his compositions remained unchanged: the unmasking of
evil and the affirmation of humanist ideals.

By now there had been peace for a quarter of a century; in
the Soviet Union the last echoes of gunfire had long since
died away. A generation which had never known war had
already grown up. Yet soldiers were still dying from old

wounds, and the hearts of those who could not forget still ached.

On September 19, 1941, Nazi troops had occupied Kiev. On the pretext of evacuation, on September 29 all the city's Jews were rounded up near a huge ravine known as Babi Yar, on the outskirts of Kiev. That same day thirty thousand people were shot there; the rest waited their turn. Day after day those who lived in the streets nearby heard measured bursts of machine-gun fire.

When the Jews had been disposed of, it was the turn of the Gypsies. After that they shot everyone indiscriminately— Ukrainians, Russians, Poles. People were shot for breeding pigeons, for wearing felt boots, for being in the streets after curfew. Hostages were taken—the first passers-by on the street—and they too were sent to Babi Yar to be shot.

Two years later, when the Red Army was returning victoriously to this place which had seen so much suffering, the Nazis began feverishly to obliterate the traces of their crimes. Excavators and bulldozers toiled in the ravine; huge trenches were dug. Hundreds of prisoners, shackled and supervised by guards, labored from dawn to dusk building furnaces in which thousands of corpses were incinerated. The prisoners knew that their turn would come later: none of them would be left alive, for what they had seen was too terrible. So they decided on a hopelessly daring attempt to escape. Of several hundred people, only four or five managed to save themselves, and it was they who told the world about the horrors of Babi Yar.

Yevgeni Yevtushenko's poem is a requiem for the innumerable victims of Nazism, anti-Semitism, and nationalism.

> And I am one silent cry
> over the many thousands of the buried;
> I am every old man killed here,
> every child killed here.

The poet was not thinking of the tragedy of Babi Yar alone. There are also references to Dreyfus, the French officer falsely accused of treason; to an unnamed little boy in Bialystok trampled to death by a drunken gang; and to Anne Frank, the young girl executed by the Nazis.

No part of me can ever forget it.

A spirit of tragedy pervades the first movement of the symphony. Heightened by the music, these resounding words ring out as a vivid conclusion to the movement:

> No Jewish blood runs in my blood,
> but I am as bitterly and hardly hated
> by every anti-Semite
> as if I were a Jew. By this
> I am a Russian.

The second movement, *Humor*, is sardonic and seethes with energy; its feeling is akin to "John Barleycorn's Round" —a symbol of life, all-conquering and perpetually renewing itself. The third movement is devoted to the women of Russia.

> These are the women of Russia,
> Our honor, judgment upon us.

The music is measured but intense, full of nobility and at times pathos.

The fourth movement introduces what was perhaps the most important theme for that period:

> In Russia fears are dying,
> Like ghosts of bygone years . . .
> Today they are far off,
> Strange now even to remember.
> The hidden fear of someone's denunciation,
> The hidden fear of the knock upon the door.

I see new fears, glimmering,
The fear of lying to one's country.
The fear that untruth will debase ideas,
Ideas that are themselves the truth.

The symphony's finale, *A Career*, is dedicated to those who did not consider career or advantage, renouncing ambition, upholding "ideas that are themselves the truth," and giving their lives for truth's eternal triumph.

In the same year, 1962, Shostakovich was accepted as a member of the Communist Party. There is evidently an underlying logic in the fact that Shostakovich turned to a theme of such acute public concern in the same year that he became a communist. This was natural for an artist who was conscious of himself as a citizen and who from his first experiments had tried to reflect in music the events around him, the life of his country and the world.

Since the Eleventh Symphony bears the title *The Year 1905* and the Twelfth *The Year 1917* some commentators have suggested that titles with symbolic dates might also be ascribed to two other symphonies: to the Seventh, *The Year 1941*, and to the Thirteenth, *The Year 1956*.

In September 1962 the annual Edinburgh Festival took place in Scotland. Apart from music, there were also films, ballets, and drama productions. Those attending the Festival were able to get to know a variety of literary works, as well as paintings. There was also the spectacular military tattoo. All this, however, was mere setting: the centerpiece of the Festival was the music of Shostakovich. Performances of almost thirty of his works were given, including the Fourth, Sixth, Ninth, Tenth, and Twelfth Symphonies, some extracts from the opera *Katerina Izmailova*, the song cycle *From Jewish Folk Poetry*, the Satires to verses by Sasha Chorny, the Violin and Cello Concertos, the Quartets, and Moussorgsky's *Khovanshchina* as orchestrated by Shostakovich. The performers were the most eminent artists from the Soviet Union and abroad; *Khovanshchina* was brought to the Festival by the Belgrade Opera. Shostakovich was present at these musical celebrations as an honored guest of the Festival. From Edinburgh he went to London, where some of his compositions were performed during "Russian Music Week."

In the mid 1950s, the Repino Composers' Retreat was opened in the Karelian Isthmus a few dozen miles from Leningrad. Over the years that followed more and more new cottages were built—modest but comfortable little houses in which composers could relax and work in peace. The houses are located right on the shore of the Gulf of Finland, spaced out in such a way that the sounds of music will not disturb the neighbors.

It was to this spot, to cottage No. 20, that Dmitri and Irina came at the end of 1962. There was a small entrance hall, a bedroom, and a bathroom. The living room had a radio and a television so that Dmitri could follow soccer matches, and there was a samovar. On summer evenings they liked to sit on the glazed veranda with its lightweight dachastyle furniture, welcoming guests or chatting with the grandchildren who lived close by in the old dacha at Komarovo and cycled over to visit. But of course the study was the main room in the house. There was a small writing table, a comfortable armchair, a sofa, and—a natural but also necessary luxury—a fine grand piano. This was all the composer needed. A communal dining room, library, and billiard room, and a hall for listening to music and watching films, were all located separately in a large building where everyone who lived at the Retreat would gather.

Shostakovich took a great liking to this place; he felt at ease there. At around nine o'clock he would go to the dining room. He breakfasted quickly, not allowing himself to be distracted, then returned to his writing table. Before lunch he took a brief break, strolling around the paths of the Retreat. He lunched punctually at two, then continued his work unless there were visitors—pupils who had an appointment or friends from Leningrad: Venyamin Basner, Isaac Glikman, Yevgeni Mravinsky or Nikolai Rabinovich. Sometimes colleagues working in the neighboring cottages would drop by to chat, listen to music, play their latest composition, or ask advice.

In the evenings Shostakovich would often go to Leningrad for a concert or the theater. His wife Irina drove the car. In his younger days Dmitri had seldom sat behind the wheel, although he had a driving license by the early 1930s. Now, with an ailing hand, it was quite impossible for him to drive.

The landmark of the following year, 1963, was *Hamlet*. It was not the first time that Shostakovich had turned to this theme. More than thirty years previously the talented producer and artist Nikolai Akimov had put on an interesting but paradoxical production of the play at the Vakhtangov Theater in Moscow. Underlying his interpretation was an idea expressed in an article by Sollertinsky on *Hamlet*. Reviewing the various ways in which the tragedy had been staged over the more than three centuries of its existence, the critic found that in European theater there had never been one single, identical interpretation of Hamlet: "There were sentimentalist Hamlets, romantic Hamlets, Byronic Hamlets, idealistic Hamlets, pessimistic Hamlets, neurotic Hamlets, etc. Yet their development had been consistent, not fortuitous, for in these types—in each new interpretation—important characteristics of the evolution of culture were reflected."

From this Sollertinsky had concluded that Soviet theaters should develop the true Shakespearean Hamlet, rather than the myth which had formed around him over the succeeding centuries—a Hamlet who would have more vitality, be more full-blooded than the subsequent philosophical interpretations of him.

> We have no description from a contemporary of Shakespeare which corresponds to any respresentation of Hamlet. I would say openly that against the background of "merry old England" a hero in the tradition of Goethe, devoid of will and full of intellectual reflections about the meaning of life, seems almost flagrantly modernist. . . . Evidently what the audience found fascinating in the tragedy was the criminal plot, which is deliberately delayed by the moments in which Hamlet reflects; bearing in mind the acting techniques of the day, it is easy to imagine the kind of emphasis given to the scenes of Hamlet's madness, his cynical jokes directed against Ophelia, and Ophelia's madness itself. . . . Hamlet's wit and the coarse jokes of the gravediggers no doubt gave rise to Homeric laughter, as did all the scenes of Hamlet's madness in general; in the England of the sixteenth and seventeenth centuries the mad were cruelly ridiculed, not romanticized . . . in other words, the theatrical content of *Hamlet* was a compound of comic scenes and scenes of horror.

Judging from surviving recollections of it, Akimov's production had been more or less along these lines. Since, however, this was not the seventeenth but the twentieth century, the production had elements of the ironic and the grotesque. Shostakovich's accompanying music had been similar in character, combining deeply tragic passages with others which are mischievous—music in which a lively and even frivolous galop gives way to a simple song, followed in turn by an episode of pure and compelling lyricism. In a review, Sollertinsky had written that Shostakovich's music was totally inseparable from the production, and that the way in which it merged with Akimov's approach was remarkable.

Now the subject arose again: the most prominent Soviet film director, Kozintsev, was making a film. Shostakovich had worked with him before, beginning with his youthful epic *New Babylon*. This was to be a seriously conceived *Hamlet* without the slightest hint of irony and with no modernization. The spirit and atmosphere of Shakespeare's time were painstakingly re-created. At the same time the director and the actor taking the part of Hamlet—the outstanding Soviet artist Innokenti Smoktunovsky—created a *Hamlet* belonging to the latter half of the twentieth century, a complex and in many ways frightening period which provokes reflection on the future destiny of mankind.

Shostakovich began work on the music with enthusiasm. The subject fulfilled an inner need which was of deep concern to him. He succeeded in writing music for the film that was integral in its approach rather than merely illustrating the individual episodes. It heightens the tragedy of the action, which may at times be obscured by various surface details. The music is, as it were, the nerve center of the film.

[1963–1966]

The autumn of 1963 saw the beginning of a very busy and restless period of months, or even years, in the composer's life. His activities were admittedly agreeable, involving the fortunes on stage of his favorite creation, the opera *Katerina Izmailova*. The opera was to be staged in many European theaters, and Shostakovich was determined to take part in the productions. On occasion this obliged him to go to almost fantastic lengths: in November he had to fly from Moscow to London, then from London to Riga, on to Moscow and then back to London—all in the space of ten days. The reason was that premières were to take place almost simultaneously in the Latvian Opera House in Riga and at Covent Garden in London.

On November 29 Shostakovich spoke by telephone to newsmen in Moscow:

> Perhaps it's true that I've flown too much in recent days. In mid-November I arrived in London to work with the staff of the Covent Garden Opera House on preparations for the première of *Katerina Izmailova*. No sooner had we got into the swing of things, so to speak, than it was time to fly to Riga. The Riga première took place on November 23. This was my first experience of artistic co-operation with the talented and indeed remarkable staff of the Latvian Opera House. I don't want to analyze the première just now (the composer is the last person who should do that), but I think the Riga production is a success.
>
> The London première was on December 2, so I had to fly

there from Riga. I did a great deal of work in a friendly atmosphere with the conductor Mr. Downes, the experienced singers, and the excellent orchestra. Although I don't know the English language well, it hasn't been too difficult for me here. First, the language of musicians can be understood without interpreters, and second, Mr. Downes knows a little Russian. But the main point has been the interest shown by the conductor, the singers, and the musicians, which ensured that we understood each other extremely well.

A production of *Katerina Izmailova* in London in English is not extraordinary. The British love our Russian music. We'll be hoping that our première will come up to the audience's expectations. I don't want to name the artists and musicians at this stage (there is a time for everything, and the British press will no doubt deal with this). But I'd like to mention that the opera has been put together with much good taste, in a truly Russian style.

So the London première will take place soon. Londoners are said to be showing great interest in it. Of course I'm not well-informed about this since I'm very busy with the rehearsals.

The composer saw in the New Year of 1964 at home among his relatives, but as early as New Year's Day he left for Yugoslavia, where another première was given at the Zagreb Opera House on January 7. Once again Shostakovich managed to be present at the final rehearsal, so as to give instructions to the performers. As always during his journeys abroad he went to concerts, seizing the opportunity to listen to music in both Zagreb and Belgrade.

In mid-January he returned to Moscow, but did not linger in the capital; his students in Leningrad were waiting for him. He spent three weeks in Repino working with his pupils and finishing the music for *Hamlet*. By February 15 he was in Gorky, a large city on the Volga where a festival devoted to his music was being held.

In February he went back to Leningrad: the Lenfilm studios were preparing *Hamlet* for release and his presence was required. Yet he still managed to tear himself away to go to Moscow for a few days: Benjamin Britten was there, and Shostakovich could not miss the opportunity of seeing him and hearing his music.

At the end of March there was a quiet week which he spent at Repino, which was still in the grip of winter and covered by snow; he enjoyed the silence. Then on March 30, after seeing *Hamlet*, he returned to Moscow but not for long, being already expected in Central Asia, where a ten-day festival of Russian music was beginning. Tashkent, Samarkand: amid the turbulent flowering of spring, there already well advanced, he entered an entirely different world of warm days and a southern carnival of bright and varied colors. Before the May Day celebrations, however, he returned to Moscow, staying three days in Leningrad, where he had to spend time with his students; he was at the dacha at Zhukovka for the first week in May. There he began writing the Tenth Quartet, dedicated to Irina. Surrounded by the peaceful landscape of the Moscow environs, with the freshly sprouting greenery of its bushes and trees and the emerald of its new grass, he had only a week to work in and to recover from nonstop traveling and constantly changing impressions.

Only one week, for he spent the next in Rostov-on-Don, where he had made guest appearances in the early 1930s and now entered yet another climate; matters concerning the Composers' Union awaited him there. On his return he finished the quartet and, after the usual visit to the Conservatory in Leningrad, met Yevtushenko. Shostakovich felt a genuine liking for the poet after their work on the Thirteenth Symphony. The composer enjoyed talking to him and followed his artistic career with interest. On this occasion the conversation concerned a further collaborative work. That, however, was yet to come, and in the meantime, in July, Shostakovich was writing his Tenth Quartet at the Dilizhan Composers' Retreat in Armenia.

Shostakovich found this establishment congenial. Opened not long before, it was situated in the mountains in a picturesque spot not far from Lake Sevan, some sixty miles from Yerevan. This was Shostakovich's second visit; he had first been there in 1963, also in July. Always sensitive to beauty and passionately fond of nature, he was overwhelmed by the surroundings and wrote enthusiastic letters to friends about the Biblical landscapes of Armenia and the bleak and savage fascination of its mountains and valleys: "You really ought to go to Dilizhan. It is unusually fine in every respect" —this from a letter to his pupil, the composer Vladislav Uspensky. In the same letter, apologizing for handwriting even more indecipherable than usual, he wrote: "I still haven't learned how to write with my left hand, but I'm giving myself plenty of practice. So far it's worked out very badly." At this time his right hand was virtually out of commission.

The composer worked fruitfully in Dilizhan. On days when he was free, his Armenian colleagues showed him their republic. He went to Yerevan and visited the studio of the remarkable artist Martiros Saryan. He saw the ancient monastery of Echmiadzin in the Gekhart ravine and admired the magnificent view of Mount Ararat from the hills around Yerevan.

On July 29 Shostakovich and his wife left Armenia. He continued his vacation and his work in Hungary at Lake Balaton. There he spent a fortnight in which he began work on a symphonic poem with voices, *The Execution of Stepan Razin*, to verses by Yevtushenko. The basis for the work was extracts from Yevtushenko's poem "The Bratsk Hydroelectric Power Station." Although the poem as a whole is devoted to the gigantic work of constructing a hydroelectric power station on one of the main rivers in Siberia, it contains episodes relating to Russian history. One of these gives an account of the Cossack hetman Stepan Razin, who led a rebellion in the seventeenth century.

Stepan Razin was one of the most colorful and striking figures in Russian history, so it is not surprising that among the people songs and legends about him abound. In the nineteenth century the Russian writer and democrat Alexander Herzen wrote of him: "Give Stenka* Razin a specific goal, give him an army instead of the Cossack poor, place him on the throne, and you have Peter the Great." Describing Razin, Herzen said that he was distinguished by "boldness, audacity, villainy, courage." This episode also fascinated Shostakovich, who followed the example of his favorite composer Moussorgsky, the author of *Boris Godunov* and *Khovanshchina*, in turning to one of the most crucial moments in Russian history.

In mid-August Shostakovich returned to Moscow, where he finished the symphonic poem. In September it was given a hearing in the composer's apartment: there were musicians present, friends of Shostakovich; also Yevtushenko and the composer's son Maxim, who by now had become a conductor.

Shostakovich's stay in Moscow was brief, however, for the regular music festival in Ufa, capital of Soviet Bashkiria, was beginning; as First Secretary of the board of the Composers' Union of the Russian Soviet Federal Socialist Republic, he had to be there. In November he again went to Leningrad where, following the première in Moscow, the Ninth and Tenth Quartets were performed. In December too he spent some days in his native city, but returned to Moscow before

* Because Razin was of humble origin, before the Revolution it was the practice to refer to him not by the full form of his name—Stepan— but by the diminutive "Stenka."

the New Year. The year 1965 found the family at the dacha in Zhukovka with Benjamin Britten, who had come to stay with them.

The new year was no more tranquil than its predecessor—indeed, it proved even more hectic. To be sure, he did not stir throughout January, spending twenty days in the neurological unit of a hospital. But by January 31 he was on a train to Vienna, where preparations were under way for the première of *Katerina Izmailova.*

The twelve days in Vienna were remarkably busy. There were, of course, rehearsals every day except Sunday. After the rehearsals, however, and the obligatory official calls, receptions, and press conferences (Shostakovich was for many years President of the Austria–Soviet Union Friendship Association), the composer still managed to spend his spare time profitably, attending Richard Strauss's *Der Rosenkavalier* at the Staatsoper; Mahler's Fifth Symphony and a Mozart concerto in performances by Viennese musicians; Lehar's *Merry Widow* and Dvořák's *Rusalka* at the Volksoper; and a concert that included a Bruckner Mass and one of the Brahms piano concertos. At a meeting with Austrian musicians of the *Gesellschaft der Freunde der Musik,* he got to know recent compositions by his Austrian fellow musicians. And of course he took walks around Vienna to see the sights and visit those places, dear to every musician, associated with Mozart, Beethoven, and Schubert.

The opera's première took place on February 12, and Shostakovich and his wife left Austria the following day. They went by train: the two days of traveling allowed them a rest. No further relaxation could be expected: immediately after his arrival in Moscow the composer flew to Kazan, where another première of *Katerina Izmailova* was given on February 17.

The whole of the next month was given over to travel. In Moscow there was a performance of *The Execution of Stepan Razin*; in Kiev, rehearsals for *Katerina Izmailova*; in Leningrad, the usual obligations to his students. All these activities were going on at the same time, yet everywhere he went Shostakovich found time to listen to music: the Eighth Symphony of Moisei Weinberg in the Great Hall of the Moscow Conservatory, *Lucia di Lammermoor* at the Kiev Opera, and a new symphony by the Ukrainian composer Lyatoshinsky at the Philharmonic.

The end of March and the beginning of April he spent in Bulgaria, where a festival of Russian music was being held at Ruse. Shostakovich was a member of a delegation headed by Tikhon Khrennikov, First Secretary of the U.S.S.R. Composers' Union. There too the first performance of a production of *Katerina Izmailova* took place on one of the days of the festival. Again the composer traveled home by train, gaining two days in which to relax. The meetings for the Lenin Prize awaited him, as did his students and the rehearsals for the opera, which was being produced at the Maly Theater Opera House.

This life on wheels, alternating between trains and hotels, continued until July, when the composer finally left for Repino. There he had just over three weeks' rest—or relative rest: he was obliged to return to Moscow for a few days, and colleagues living near Repino called every day, seeking advice or help or merely paying friendly visits.

The Shostakoviches spent the first half of August in Byelorussia, in the famous Byelovezhskaya Forest. In the silent depths of the woods the composer felt himself relieved of cares for the first time in this extremely busy year. This, at last, was a real vacation.

The fortnight passed quickly. By August 15 tickets for Moscow had already been booked. But bad news awaited him in the capital: Vasili Shirinsky, second violinist of the Beethoven Quartet and a friend with whom Shostakovich had maintained a close artistic and personal association over several decades, had died.

The Beethoven Quartet was the ensemble to which the composer had entrusted all the first performances of his quartets. In writing them he could count on musicians whom he knew well and of whom he was very fond, musicians on whose individuality and creative style he could rely. The death of Vasili Shirinsky, then, was more than the loss of a friend: there was the danger that a magnificent and unique musical ensemble would perish. "We all take leave of life sooner or later," Shostakovich said to Dmitri Tsyganov, the Quartet's leader, "but the Beethoven Quartet must go on for fifty years, for a hundred years. It is your duty to ensure that the Quartet remains at the high level it should maintain, even when its senior members gradually depart."

The composer dedicated his Eleventh Quartet to the memory of Vasili Shirinsky. It was not written until the following year, 1966, however, since Shostakovich had been wholly preoccupied by outside matters and obligations at the time.

His students were waiting for him in Leningrad, but first there was work to be done in Kiev, where the orchestra of the Kiev Opera House was recording the sound track of a film version of *Katerina Izmailova*. On September 24, the day before his birthday, the composer wrote to Vladislav Uspensky:

> It's possible that I won't be able to get to Leningrad on October 3 as agreed. If so, I'll arrive a few days later. I'll let you know in due course when I'm coming. I'd like you to arrange our meetings as follows: on the first day I'll see you and Tishchenko. On the second, Bibergan and Nogovitsyn; and on the third, whoever wishes to see me. I was worn out by business in Moscow, and today I've fled to the dacha.

There are good things among the new compositions. Wein-berg's cantata is very good. Levitan has produced a very attractive Sonatina for Violin and Piano. It's been a pleasure getting to know these pieces.

He managed to travel to Leningrad in mid-October, but had to return to Moscow at the end of the month: a meeting of the Meyerhold Committee was being convened. Shostako-vich was a member of the committee and, revering as he did the memory of the great director, would not have dreamed of missing any of its meetings. Before this he managed to snatch a few days' rest at the dacha in Zhukovka. But his pupils in Leningrad continued to occupy his thoughts. In a letter to that city he wrote: "I think that form plays an enormous part in opera—no less than in a symphony. Otherwise what may result is not opera but a pot-pourri."

November began in Ioshkar-Ola, the capital of the Mariisk Autonomous Republic, where Shostakovich had to deal with matters concerning the Composers' Union. He returned to Moscow on the morning of November 7, a public holiday, and the next two weeks went by fairly quietly except for anxieties about his son Maxim's concert in the Great Hall of the Conservatory. On November 22 they celebrated the birthday of Benjamin Britten, who was visiting the Soviet Union at the time. A concert of his music was given in Tchaikovsky Hall, and there was also a banquet. During the last days of November there were concerts at the Composers' Center which Shostakovich assiduously attended. At one of these a performance was given of the Second Symphony of Orest Yevlakhov, a Leningrad composer who had once been Shostakovich's pupil.

The frantic pace of the year continued into December: he had to go to Leningrad for two days. A week in mid-month was spent in Budapest, where *Katerina Izmailova* was being staged. As usual there were receptions, visits, press conferences, and concerts to attend, apart from the rehearsals. He also met Kodály, the *doyen* of Hungarian music. After Budapest he had to go to the city of Gorky for performances of his Thirteenth Symphony on December 24 and 25.

The family greeted the New Year, as usual, at the dacha. It brought no change in the pattern of his life: the whirlwind continued. On January 12, 1966, he was in Kiev. On the 15th, already back in Moscow, he flew to Novosibirsk. He had not been in the city since the far-off days of the war, when Mravinsky had performed the Seventh Symphony there. Now in Novosibirsk itself and in Akademgorod—a settlement of scientists along the shore of the Obsk dam— there were performances of the Thirteenth Symphony. On January 20, after the Siberian première, Shostakovich flew back to Moscow.

Part of February he spent in Leningrad, at Repino. He wrote the Eleventh Quartet in memory of Vasili Shirinsky, and took part in a television broadcast on Sollertinsky. The trip to Novosibirsk undoubtedly reopened an old wound. Remembering his long-lost friend, the composer said: "Working on my new compositions, I always think: what would Ivan Ivanovich have said about this? I feel that the best way to perpetuate the shining memory of Ivan Ivanovich Sollertinsky, an outstanding Soviet musician, is to work with passion and ardor so that Soviet musical life may continue to flourish."

The month of March Shostakovich spent in Moscow. The 30th saw the beginning of the Twenty-eighth Congress of the Communist Party, which the composer attended as a delegate. When the Congress ended he went to Leningrad for some days at the Composers' Union, returning promptly to attend the Lenin and State Prize Committee meetings from April 12 to 19.

On the evening of April 19 a train took him to the Crimea, where he stayed in the Oreanda sanatorium near Yalta. Here he wrote his Second Cello Concerto. But he was not feeling well; a cough interfered with his breathing, and his doctors prescribed inhalation treatment. Shostakovich meticulously followed the treatment, but to no avail: the cough would not go away. Other troubles unconnected with the illness had by now become chronic, but he paid no attention to them. He thought that if he rested everything would pass and be forgotten.

In mid-May, after his return to Moscow, he went to Volgograd, where the Thirteenth Symphony was being performed. The occasion upset him: the performance did not go well. Returning again to Moscow on May 23, he went on the following day to hear Britten's *War Requiem* in concert and directly afterward left for Leningrad. In Leningrad, it was uncharacteristically stifling and hot for the month of May. The composer felt unwell, he was troubled by heartburn; once again, though, he considered this of no importance and refused to slacken his pace or alter his schedule.

On May 25 he and Maxim visited the Piskarevsky Memorial Cemetery with its eternal flame and the inscription: "No one is forgotten, nothing is forgotten"; there, buried side by side, lay hundreds of thousands of victims of the 1941–44 siege. During the next few days he met with friends and listened to music. Then on May 28 there was a concert of his works in the Small Hall of the Philharmonic. During the night of May 28–29, however, his condition became serious. The doctors diagnosed a heart attack.

[1966]

The first week passed like an agonizing dream—hours and days between life and death, immobility, almost complete isolation. Around him were none of the familiar faces, none of the usual bustle and movement. With him was only his wife, Irina, constantly present, solicitous and untiring. Doctors, nurses, and orderlies came and went, but Shostakovich was agonizingly shy with strangers and Irina preferred to take care of him herself.

After a few days his condition improved and visitors were allowed into the hospital. The first to arrive was Maxim, distraught and exhausted. He was due to leave the city—he was expected on business in Moscow—but could not go without seeing his father and making sure that the worst was over.

Nikolai Rabinovich came on the same day. A fine conductor and a serious and thoughtful musician, he had been an old friend of Shostakovich and Sollertinsky. By tradition he recorded all Shostakovich's film music, beginning in 1929 with the memorable film *Girl Alone*. There had been a great deal of artistic collaboration between them: the film *The Golden Mountains*, for which the composer had been invited to write a score immediately after completing *Girl Alone*; *The Passer-by*, with its famous *Song about a Passer-by* to the spirited and resonant lines of the talented poet Boris Kornilov; the memorable trilogy on the Petrograd working boy Maxim which had occupied his thoughts for five whole years; and *Volochaev Days*, a film which so interested Shostakovich that at one time he had thought seriously of writing an opera on the subject.

This is not to mention all the films for which Shostakovich wrote music even in the prewar years, with Nikolai Rabinovich always at his side, ever alert and quick to grasp the composer's ideas without words or explanations. Their collaboration had continued after the war, from the mid-1940s on. There were films about the grim days that had gone by: *The Young Guard*, *Meeting on the Elbe*, and *The Fall of Berlin*. Others were devoted to noted Russians of the past: *Belinsky*, about the great Russian critic, known as "the furious Vissarion," who left a legacy of brilliant studies of Russian literature of the first half of the nineteenth century; and *Michurin*, which concerned an agronomist and breeder who introduced many new strains of fruit trees, "Michurin's varieties," yielding appetizing frost- and drought-resistant fruit—trees that were cultivated throughout the country.

Still more films had followed: *The Unforgettable Year 1919*, *The Gadfly*, *Five Days, Five Nights*, and finally the most important of their co-operative ventures: Kozintsev's *Hamlet*. It seemed quite recently that they had spent many hours together working on *Hamlet*. In the fall of 1962 Shostakovich had visited Rabinovich's dacha in the Baltic village of Ust-Narva and they had talked of many things—the past, old friends, music. They had tastes in common: not for nothing had they both experienced the potent influence of Ivan Sollertinsky in their youth. Both had a broad range of appreciation in art—"from Bach to Offenbach," as Sollertinsky had once joked—and both worshiped Mahler.

In his archive the conductor cherished a valuable letter from Shostakovich in which the composer wrote:

Dear Nikolai Semyonovich,

Yesterday [January 3] at nine o'clock in the evening I listened to your performance of Mahler's Third Symphony on the radio.* It was broadcast on Leningrad's channel three. Presumably it was a recording. Despite certain shortcomings inherent in radio broadcasts, the symphony and your performance made a tremendous impression on me. I'm no critic and don't concern myself with analysis. I can only say I was totally absorbed by the symphony. . . .

Everything sounded splendid, the orchestra, choirs, soloists (the female soloist, the orchestral musicians, especially the French horn and the trombone—and indeed all the others, too). Nothing went wrong with either the interpretation or the performance.

I extend warm thanks to you for this Third Symphony. Keep well and happy and carry on in the same spirit.

I shake your hand warmly.

> Yours,
> D. Shostakovich

Several days later Mravinsky called on the sick man. He too had matters to talk and reminisce about. There was the première of the Fifth Symphony, their work together on the Seventh in distant Novosibirsk, and their last meetings with Sollertinsky. There was also Mravinsky's introduction to the Eighth and its dedication, of which the celebrated conductor was no less proud than of the high honors he had been accorded.

The composer's sister Maria Dmitrievna, the eldest of the large Shostakovich family, began to call. She too had not been well. The privations and experiences of the siege had had their effect.

The most frequent visitor to the hospital was Isaac Glikman. A noted theater director in Leningrad and former assistant to Sollertinsky in the Philharmonic, he had become acquainted with Shostakovich through his chief and they had

---

* Rabinovich had recorded this monumental symphony, so difficult to perform, with a student orchestra from the Leningrad Conservatory and an amateur chorus.

grown to be close friends. Even in the 1930s they had been together a lot. Glikman would go to all the rehearsals before the performance of Shostakovich's works, and would self-sacrificingly accompany him to soccer matches. He went with him to the dacha. Shostakovich liked him for his wit, liveliness, and resourcefulness. Later he began to help the composer with his affairs, especially with foreign correspondence.

Shostakovich, always punctilious, insisted on conferring official status on this assistance. Hence the appearance of a curious document which the Union of Workers in the Arts had received on May 19, 1936: "Attestation: Given to Comrade I. D. Glikman, to confirm that he is working in the capacity of personal secretary to the composer D. D. Shostakovich." Glikman remained a "secretary" until the early months of the war, although from 1939 on, as a teacher in the Leningrad Conservatory, he had become Shostakovich's colleague.

The war years had separated them. Of course they wrote letters, but these could not take the place of a living relationship. So when in 1942 a request for the score of the Seventh Symphony arrived from Tashkent, the city to which the Conservatory had been evacuated, Shostakovich replied affirmatively, adding a request that Glikman be sent for the score. Glikman spent a month with Shostakovich while the score and the orchestral parts were being transcribed. The two friends could talk to their hearts' content, in recompense for the long months of separation.

Later Glikman was to receive a grief-stricken letter:

February 13, 1944. Moscow.

Dear Isaac Davidovich,

Accept my sincerest condolences on the death of our closest and dearest friend Ivan Ivanovich Sollertinsky. No words can express the grief which tears at my whole being. Let his memorial be our love for him and our faith in his genius and his astonishing devotion to the art to which he gave his splendid life—music.

D. Shostakovich

After Sollertinsky's death Glikman had been Shostakovich's closest friend. Their firm friendship was lifelong; it did not matter that they lived in different cities. There was a regular correspondence, and every time Shostakovich came to Leningrad he met his friend. Their joint work kept them together. On the composer's insistence Glikman became editor and consultant for the films *Cheryomushki*, *Katerina Izmailova*, and *Hamlet*.

When he was preparing a second edition of *Katerina Izmailova*, Shostakovich had asked his friend to take a careful look at the libretto and consider what might need changing in it. Glikman began work, bearing in mind the productions he had seen in 1935 and the audience's reaction to particular passages in the text. So the new edition appeared, with the full approval of the composer. Again, when the Leningrad choreographer Konstantin Boyarsky had the idea of creating a ballet based on Shostakovich's Tenth Symphony, it was Glikman who wrote a libretto for it.

Yet what was most important was that for more than forty years they were fond of each other, were spiritually akin and true to the memory of Sollertinsky and to their friendship with him. At one time all three had been close friends, with a constant mutual understanding. For more than twenty years only two members of this triumvirate remained, and now the fateful line dividing the living from those who survived only in human memory had all but been crossed.

Life was gradually returning. The threads linking Shostakovich to the world about him were being restored. He had spent four months languishing within the walls of the hospital. Only at the beginning of August 1966 did the doctors allow him to leave. He was sent to the excellent sanatorium at Melnichny Ruchei near Leningrad, but was still not permitted to make a longer journey.

He passed the time reading books and in leisurely conversation with friends—and, of course, watching television when soccer matches were being broadcast. This passion of his early years had in no way diminished, having taken root and become a habitual and necessary part of his life. Even during the evacuation from besieged Leningrad he had managed to take with him his "scorebook" containing detailed records of the performance of Leningrad soccer players in the national championships, their standing in the leagues, the results of matches against rival teams, and the names of those who scored goals.

Sports had revived as the war came to an end, and Shostakovich, already resident in Moscow, had gone regularly to the stadium to support his favorite Leningrad teams. In 1944 the journalist Mikhail Alexandrov went with the composer to a soccer match in which the *Zenit* team was playing. He described the occasion:

> The match proved most interesting. The Leningrad team played superbly. They attacked from right and left on a broad front persistently and, one might even say, with inspiration. The Moscow spectators gave warm support to the Leningrad players, consciously or unconsciously paying tribute to the sportsmen of the heroic city. I looked at Dmitri Dmitrievich, who was hemmed in by bystanders applauding and shouting excitedly. How can I describe it? Honestly, he was as happy as a small boy! He sat silently, wide-eyed with ardent enthusiasm behind his thick lenses.
>
> Then suddenly it began to pour. In an instant the stands began to rustle with newspapers. But what use were newspapers against such a furious downpour? In a minute or two

we were completely soaked. I suggested, "Perhaps we should leave, Dmitri Dmitrievich, and take shelter somewhere until it's over?" Large, reproachful eyes glanced at me from behind the wet lenses of his spectacles: "What? How could you even think of it? Anyway, just look over there, that patch of sky's turning blue!"

Zenit won that game. We came back from the stadium in a dense crowd of talkative young people discussing an interesting and hard-fought match.

"Superb!" Dmitri Dmitrievich kept saying, greatly delighted by what he had just witnessed.

Many people were aware of his passion for sports. Journalists interviewing him sometimes asked him not only about music but about soccer as well.

Indeed, not long previously, on his return from Budapest in January, he had met with a correspondent from *Izvestiya*. After questions about *Katerina Izmailova*, his creative plans, and his concerns of the past year, the conversation turned to sports—to soccer and chess, in which Shostakovich also took a lively interest, and not merely as a fan. "You've never lost your passion for these activities?" asked the correspondent. Six months later Shostakovich could still recall his reply: "Not at all. Even now I'm trying to find time for these two games. I go to soccer matches. I love soccer and think I understand the subtleties of the game. And I'm very fond of chess: it combines both art and science. It gives me relaxation and inspiration."

Shostakovich had been keen on chess since childhood. At the age of ten or eleven he was already playing very well. Once his father took him to the cinema, where before the showing enthusiasts of the game were sitting playing chess. Dmitri was brought to one of the chess tables, someone approached . . . fascinated by the game, the boy did not even pay close attention to his opponent. It turned out afterward that his opponent had been the legendary Alekhine himself.

After a month in the sanatorium Shostakovich moved to the Repino Retreat that he liked so much, and into his old cottage, No. 20. His strength was now returning. Gradually he got back into his regular working routine, although that routine was certainly not as intense as it had been two or three years before. His pupils began to visit. Once again there were things to do, there was music, and he found himself engaged in interesting conversations. They talked not only about music but about everything that interested and excited him. One of the composer's closest pupils, Boris Tishchenko, recalled:

> His views were fixed and precise. He disliked half-heartedness and indecisiveness in anything—in opinions, tastes, even minor matters. What he said was concrete and specific: every thought was expressed in a strict yet ample literary form—sometimes it was even a short story. Shostakovich was hostile to diffuse, abstract discussions and platitudes. There was no magniloquence, no pathos, everything was specific and well-rounded. "How can you pronounce 'mama' at the pace of a tongue-twister? You can't!" he once said à propos of one of our compositions.
>
> "You can't say 'I wrote this to a text.'—An announcement or a declaration can have a text, but surely poetry can't be a text?"

It was not only verse that Shostakovich himself set to music. "It's all the same to me—verse or prose," he affirmed. "There's no difference. *Katerina Izmailova* has the most prosaic and mundane text. I have to feel the musical language, the character, the concealed meaning which brings me to an awareness of both the musical intonation and the musical characterization. It's interesting to try to convey in music different kinds of text, many different moods."

This must have been why in his work the composer used

such varied literary sources as the poems of Pushkin, Japanese poetry, lines by Yevtushenko, and later verses by Blok, Tsvetaeva, and Michelangelo. Besides all this, he set to music the satires of Sasha Chorny, the prose of Gogol and Leskov, and even humorous extracts from the popular satirical weekly *Krokodil*!

Shostakovich wrote one vocal work to his own words, the *Preface to My Collected Works and Some Observations on This Preface*. It ends with a tune incorporating his DSCH signature. This is the only instance in the composer's work where it is heard in a humorous, or rather ironic, context.

Shostakovich had a keen sense of humor, but it was subtle, unconventional, and very idiosyncratic. It is worth quoting the whole text of the *Preface* to give an impression of this unique work. It is a joke in the form of a paraphrase of a well-known poem by Pushkin:

> All in one breath I scribble a page
> And heed this piping with indifferent ear.
> Then to torment the world's attention
> I go to print and damnation!

There follows a surprising signature, longer than the *Preface* itself: "Dmitri Shostakovich, national artist of the U.S.S.R. A great many other honorary titles. First Secretary of the Composers' Union of the RSFSR, plain ordinary Secretary of the U.S.S.R. Composers' Union. Also a large number of other highly responsible duties and functions." As a musical joke, it is a rare example of self-mockery directed against arrogance and a false concept of prestige; it appeals for humility and simplicity.

The *Preface* was written in 1966, but some decades earlier Shostakovich had also been able to take an ironic view of himself. In his letters one frequently runs across such words as these: "Before the concert the composer gave a talk about

Ukrainian musical life. In the whole talk I could grasp only one word: Shostakovich. A neighbor amiably gave me to understand that the name was uttered in an unflattering context." (From a letter relating a visit to Kiev in 1930.)

Or, in an account of guest appearances in Rostov-on-Don at more or less the same time: "My tails give me the appearance of an elegant flunky. Several times I found myself saying "What can I do for you?" instead of "Hello" or "Good-by."

In 1934 Shostakovich wrote Sollertinsky from the Retreat at Polenovo: "Dear Ivan Ivanovich, The weather is rainy, it's muddy outside. I have to sit indoors or on the balcony. The scenery is remarkably fine, but my mind is vacant, and if you tapped me on the forehead you'd hear only a hollow, wooden sound."

Recalled Boris Tishchenko:

> Dmitri disliked coarse or salacious humor. He made great demands of humor, often finding things funny that we had passed over, unnoticing.
>
> A remarkably good and uncompromising person, laughing, smiling, yet sardonic, suffering, even groaning as if from some wound to the heart, and at the same time tender and thoughtful—that's the kind of man he was. He had a great love of nature. He would talk enthusiastically about his trip to the virgin Byelovezhskaya Forest, describing the behavior of the European bison and the wild boar. He loved cats and dogs. Even in them, however, he could not condone unkind actions.
>
> "There are rogues even among dogs. Our dog bit a kitten to death. And it wasn't as if he were hungry—he did it purely for mischief. I sent him out for twenty-four hours."

In all his meetings with his pupils, music of course was the center of attention. Sviridov's *Songs of Kursk*, Weinberg's

Sixth Symphony, and Britten's *War Requiem* and chamber operas were heard at the classes.

Shostakovich had no liking for highly colored, florid music. Although he valued the work of Stravinsky very much and considered him the greatest of twentieth-century composers, he was not overfond of the *Firebird* or the *Rite of Spring*. Nor did he approve of Rimsky-Korsakov's *Scheherezade*, although he deeply respected the other works and the personality of this remarkable musician.

He loved Alban Berg; talked delightedly of Prokofiev's operas *The Love for Three Oranges, War and Peace,* and *Semyon Kotko*; and paid great attention to the work of his colleagues. He was also most concerned that his pupils should be true professionals. One of them recalled a remark of Shostakovich's:

> "You must be able to write straight into the score in ink, without a piano."
> "But what if there's a mistake?" one of us asked.
> "You'll think before writing down the note."

Perhaps there were times when he thought that the young people so intently listening to him would be his last pupils, that not much time remained and he must contrive to transmit to those before him all that he considered important, everything he had thought over and gained through suffering in his long artistic career. And he remembered former pupils who had long since become important musicians in their own right.

Apart from his Leningrad pupils of the prewar years there had been Revol Bunin, his only student in the first months after he moved to Moscow; then the Azerbaijani Kara Karaev, who developed into a very interesting composer; and many others who had since become teachers and educators.

Today it is not merely Shostakovich's musical "children"

who live and work in the U.S.S.R.: there are grandchildren, great-grandchildren, and even great-great-grandchildren. They are to be found not only in Leningrad and Moscow but in other Russian cities as well, and in other republics. There is a whole Shostakovich school of composition which grew out of what had once been a handful of pupils.

It was not difficult to continue the classes while living at Repino. Young musicians were delighted to come visit their mentor. But the time for departure was drawing near and Shostakovich, who had always taken a very responsible attitude to his duties, began to worry. He wrote to Yevlakhov in Leningrad: "Dear Orest Alexandrovich, Yesterday I had a talk with Gabaraev and Nogovitsyn. I ask you to look after them and help them finish their score. I won't be able to come to Leningrad in the near future. My legs are giving me trouble."

This was indeed a further trial: the chronic illness which had first appeared seven years before had grown progressively worse. Each month his right hand functioned less well. He could raise it now only with difficulty; while convalescing, he supported it with his left. Furthermore, his legs too were proving noticeably less responsive.

In September he went back to Moscow. Immediately upon his return he took an active part in the rehearsals of the Cello Concerto. It was given its première on September 25, on the composer's sixtieth birthday.

At precisely that time the film of *Katerina Izmailova*—the screen version of Shostakovich's opera—was released for showing in Soviet cinemas. Millions were able to see this masterly work, one of the greatest operas.

Shostakovich resolutely declined to take part in any elaborate birthday celebrations. He simply could not have endured a long and exhausting ceremony: his heart had not regained sufficient strength. He was probably relieved to have good reasons for turning down an official celebration. Modest, retiring, loathing all ostentation, he always felt very uncomfortable when he had to take part—especially as the chief dignitary present—in any kind of formal ceremonies or honorific celebrations. How much better to gather together in a closely knit group—his wife, children, grandchildren, and two or three close friends! That was how he spent the day, with the première and a festive family dinner.

Of course he received congratulations—from colleagues in the Soviet Union and abroad, from performing musicians and music lovers, from acquaintances and strangers. For thousands of people the name of Shostakovich was not merely that of a composer who had written particular works: it was a symbol of what was noblest, boldest, and most honest in art, a symbol of conscience, civic spirit, and honor.

Several times a day the mailman brought letters and telegrams to Nezhdanova Street in Moscow. Their cordial and kindly messages gladdened him and warmed his heart. Aram Khachaturian sent a touching letter: "Today I recall our first meeting and our friendship, which began more than three decades ago. Yet even so I think I got to know you too late. I regret that the bustle of life has not allowed us more frequent contact, for to associate with you is to be enriched."

Leopold Stokowski wrote to the composer: "Together with millions of other music lovers I wish to express, on Shostakovich's sixtieth birthday, my cordial and deep gratitude for the stimulating, beautiful and powerful music he has given the world, and to wish him good health and safe-keeping. We all look forward to his latest inspired compositions." And Henri Sauguet echoed the conductor's words: "I want to express the wish that *le glorieux* Dmitri Shostakovich will continue for many more years to bestow upon the world his noble and splendid music, embodying the spirit of the great Soviet people."

It was not only to the composer himself that letters, greetings, and articles were sent. Many at this time wanted to share their recollections of him and their thoughts about his music. Their memories were as varied as the people themselves. Here are the words of the *doyen* of Armenian artists, Martiros Saryan:

> What attracts artists working in different fields to each other? Simple human affection? No, it is obviously something much deeper that brings them together, something that is not always possible to define.
>
> When I listen to Shostakovich's music, its underlying literary meaning is unimportant to me. What most attracts me is something almost impossible to define in literary terms—the musical thought itself. Often words seem to diminish the content—to impoverish and confine it. It is remarkable that the world has music capable of expressing those aspects of an individual's inner world inaccessible to every other form of art. Literature, music, painting, philosophy—all come into contact with each other, and each at the same time has a content unique to itself. Together, they reflect the richness of man's spiritual world. The music of Shostakovich always brings me back to these thoughts.

There were other articles—by an actor, a professor of mathematics, a shipyard worker. All expressed gratitude to the composer for his wonderful art, and the hope that with new and magnificent works he would continue for many years to give pleasure to those who admired his music.

Although there was no elaborate birthday celebration, Shostakovich felt exhausted after a few days in Moscow. The Shostakoviches decided they should leave the capital. They spent October and November at the dacha, far from the noise and bustle of Moscow. They visited the city rarely—usually when Dmitri had to be examined by his doctor. It was the first time in a long while that, living in silence away from the city, he was neither working nor composing. And for the first time in recent years he did not go to his graduate students in Leningrad: instead, they came to him at the end of November, and Shostakovich worked with them in his Moscow apartment.

In December, however, this seclusion came to an end. The composer was delighted to feel his strength returning. Once again urgent daily business awaited him—rehearsals, concerts, listening to music at the Composers' Union, and first nights at the theater.

Benjamin Britten visited Moscow at the end of December and joined the Shostakovich family to see in the new year, 1967, at their dacha.

[1967–1969]

The year began at a frenzied pace, with interesting concerts and stage productions which all Moscow was heatedly discussing. Almost every day Shostakovich was hurrying off somewhere, meeting large numbers of people, absorbing new impressions, and worrying. Yet every day he also spent long hours in a comfortable armchair watching television: as before, he did not miss a single ice-hockey or soccer match. He would neatly enter the results in a notebook and draw up complicated tables. Like crossword puzzles, this was his relaxation, as were games of patience, to which he had been devoted since his early years. The months passed without incident until May, when the Shostakoviches went to Repino for a fortnight. Here at last he could compose.

The Second Concerto for Violin and Orchestra was written. On May 20, already back in Moscow, he wrote to David Oistrakh: "Dear Dodik, I've finished a new violin concerto. I was thinking of you when I wrote it. I want to show you the concerto, though it's terribly difficult for me to play these days. I'll be very happy if the concerto pleases you, and if you'll play it my happiness will be beyond description. If you have no objection, I'd like to dedicate the concerto to you."

Oistrakh gratefully accepted the dedication and began learning the concerto as soon as time permitted. By July he could inform the composer, who was once again at Repino, that work was progressing successfully. The first performance was scheduled for the fall.

The Shostakoviches spent August in their beloved Byelovezhshaya state park. It was quiet and comfortable in the secluded little hotel. Morning began with Dmitri glancing through the program of the day's radio broadcasts, noting the music and sports sections, which determined the day's agenda. No interesting broadcast was missed: the composer listened with unflagging attention to everything that could be heard on the air—the music of the past, concerts by visiting musicians from abroad, new recordings, concerts of the latest Soviet music.

Thoroughly rested, full of strength and plans for work Shostakovich returned to Moscow on August 22. There, however, he broke a leg and was taken to the hospital, where he found it impossible to reestablish a proper working routine. He celebrated his birthday in the hospital, and began work there on his next opus—songs to verses by Alexander Blok for voice, violin, cello, and piano.

During these years Shostakovich turned more and more to poetry and was increasingly inspired by the verse of different periods. From his early years he had passionately loved Russian literature. He read Gogol, Chekhov, Leskov, Saltykov-Shchedrin, and of course Dostoevsky constantly. His children recall how he made them read *The Brothers Karamazov*; he used to check how much they had read each day. We should remember the part played by Gogol in his work and perhaps also in forming his personality. The composer also returned constantly to Chekhov, and in his last years he dreamed of writing an opera based on Chekhov's *The Black Monk*. But this was prose—to poetry he had paid less attention. Perhaps there had been no such tradition at home and he had simply had no opportunity to become interested in poetry. When previously he had needed texts in verse for his ideas, as for example in the Second and Third Symphonies, he had turned to whatever came to hand, often regardless of quality.

In recent years, however, volumes of poems had begun to appear in the household more and more. Shostakovich would see the slim volumes of Blok, Tsvetaeva, Akhmatova, Yevtushenko, Voznesensky, and younger poets on the shelves and tables, his hand would reach out for them, and musical ideas would begin to germinate.

This was the case, for example, with Alexander Blok. Shostakovich was attracted by those lines of the poet conveying the instability and the vague, involuntary anxiety characteristic of the Russian intelligentsia at the beginning of the century. The theme of the poems he set to music is the understanding of the inner meaning of the artist's life and the life of his country. There are seven of them: "Ophelia's Song," "Hamayun the Prophet Bird," "We Were Together," "The City Sleeps," "The Storm," "Secret Signs," and "Music." For his settings Shostakovich wrote a suite for voices and instruments. The last number, *Music*, became the climax toward which everything is directed; it is remarkable for its sublimity and beauty, being at once a summation and a program—the artist's credo.

Shostakovich was already finishing the suite at the dacha. On October 12 he had been discharged from the hospital. His leg was still in plaster and he found it difficult to move: even on crutches his arms, weak from many years of illness, could not support his frame. He was forced to get a wheelchair to move around the apartment. Even so, at the end of October he managed with great difficulty to attend the première of the Second Violin Concerto.

Afterward he had to go back into the hospital to have the cast removed and to learn how to walk. There the good news reached him of the brilliant Leningrad première of the Cello Concerto. This was an occasion out of the ordinary: the oldest higher institute of music in the country was observing the sixtieth birthday of its student and professor. The soloist had been accompanied by an orchestra of students conducted by their longstanding mentor and professor, Nikolai Rabinovich.

The following summer Shostakovich, true to his old love of travel, made yet another trip, one which had long been planned. With his wife he visited the scenic sites of the Russian North—Lakes Ladoga and Onega, the Kizhi National Park, and Valaam Island. Together with the rivers Svir and Neva and many other smaller lakes and rivers, Lakes Ladoga and Onega make up a system similar to the American Great Lakes. Their boundless smooth surfaces leave an unforgettable impression of grandeur, while their strikingly picturesque islands are covered with thick coniferous forests and strewn with huge boulders.

Unique examples of the wooden architecture of the Russian North have been preserved on one of these islands in the middle of Lake Onega: churches hewn by ax from timber and built without a single nail; huts ornamented with a lacework of wooden carvings; and peasant farm buildings. In recent years the most noteworthy buildings from European Russia had been moved to the island, to create the Kizhi National Architectural Park. This was the region that Shostakovich went to see. On the way back by train he visited the island of Valaam on Lake Ladoga, a notably beautiful island with an ancient wooden monastery.

The composer had set off on his journey to the northern lakes from Repino, where he had spent August. There the

195

Violin Sonata was written. He wrote it as a gift for David Oistrakh on the occasion of this remarkable musician's sixtieth birthday on September 30, 1968.

The following year an original and daring idea arose in the composer's mind. It had in fact germinated much earlier, at the time in 1962 when Shostakovich had begun orchestrating Moussorgsky's song cycle *Songs and Dances of Death*. The composer had been most enthusiastic about his task and had observed that this splendid work's only shortcoming was its brevity. There are, after all, four sections in the *Songs and Dances of Death*. It had then occurred to him: why not take heart and continue the piece? However, the time had evidently not yet come for carrying out the plan: other ideas and other themes were preoccupying him. Besides, the circumstances of his life inclined him to an optimistic view of things.

Did the turning point come perhaps in 1966? During the long months of illness Shostakovich must have reflected on life and death. He had long since begun to meditate on the subject; images of destruction and death, and the immortality which overcomes death, had appeared in his music. Now, in the twilight of his days, all these thoughts were taking on a special coloring and becoming more personal. From this there came into being an astonishing symphony for soprano, bass, and chamber orchestra based on verses by Federico García Lorca, Guillaume Apollinaire, Wilhelm Küchelbecker, and Rainer Maria Rilke.

The symphony has eleven movements or scenes. It evokes an extremely rich and varied world: a tavern in sultry Andalusia; a lonely crag at a bend in the river Rhine; a cell in a French prison; Pushkin's St. Petersburg; and the trenches with bullets whistling overhead. It also has varied heroes: the Lorelei, a bishop, knights, a suicide, the Zaporozhian Cossacks, a woman who has lost the one she loved, a prisoner, Death.

The overall cast of the music is sorrowful, ranging from a restrained intensity to raging and frenzied tragedy. In essence it is a protest against all that shatters human souls, destinies, and lives, against violence, oppression, and tyranny. "I want the audience to leave after a performance of the symphony with the thought that life is beautiful," said the composer. He dedicated this Fourteenth Symphony to Benjamin Britten.

After its first performance the writer Marietta Shaginian, a knowledgeable and sensitive judge of music, wrote:

For almost two thousand years mankind has been acquainted with the ritual music which has become known as "the Passion of our Lord." This was originally church music but, like the image of the Madonna in painting, which became an archetype of motherhood, over the centuries this musical form has undergone a pronounced change. The simple, worldly substance of human ordeals and sufferings has made itself apparent through the cloak of liturgy. Major composers have written music for the Passion. . . .

The Fourteenth Symphony—I would like to call it the first "Passion of Man" of the new era—shows convincingly how much our time needs a deeper interpretation of spiritual contradictions and a tragic understanding of the mental experiences ("the Passion") which constitute the ordeal through which mankind is passing. . . .

The poems chosen by Shostakovich contain nothing resembling a struggle against death as such or a protest *against death in general.* They all speak of *unnatural,* exceptional, *premature, monstrous* death, and such death should properly be seen as *destruction,* brought about by the horrors of a life which is unnatural, criminal, disfigured, and corrupted by violence.

197

The Fourteenth Symphony was composed in the hospital, where Shostakovich remained from January 13 through February 22, 1969. Unlike those occasions when going into the hospital is a matter of unexpected necessity—as with a fracture or a heart attack—this time his stay in the neurological unit had been foreseen: the progress of the illness required periodic hospital treatment. So Shostakovich entered the hospital calmly, provided with everything he needed: manuscript paper, notebooks, and a bed-table which would enable him to write comfortably. But he was greatly distressed when shortly afterward the hospital was put in quarantine, and the relatives and friends who normally visited him were no longer admitted; he was then obliged to communicate entirely in writing.

Work went well in the isolation of the hospital. Initially the days passed by imperceptibly, but gradually the solitude began to be oppressive. He missed the living contact with his friends and the living sound of music. On the very day of his discharge he went to the Great Hall of the Conservatory, where the rehearsals of a new piece by Moisei Weinberg were commencing. Weinberg was one of the musicians closest to Shostakovich. A fine pianist, he was acutely responsive to Shostakovich's music, and for this reason the composer usually demonstrated his new orchestral works to friends, colleagues, and performers by playing them with Weinberg in piano arrangements for four hands. Their performances were remarkable: they played as one person, and in expressiveness, richness of dynamics, and even tone-coloring the grand piano not only yielded nothing to the orchestral sound but sometimes surpassed it. Shostakovich had a high opinion of Weinberg's music, considering it talented and original. He never missed concerts at which it was played, and on this occasion too he was present at both the rehearsals and the première.

Later he began giving concrete form to the Fourteenth. One day in spring the composer invited his friends over to get to know the new work. He played it himself, although this was made very difficult by the condition affecting his hands. He played the voice parts rather quietly, but expressively, and it was clear that the work was very dear to him.

After he had finished and everyone had moved from the study to the dining room for tea, Shostakovich remarked in passing that he had been unable to sleep for some nights after handing over the manuscript to the copyist: the whole time he was "playing over" the music to himself, making sure he could reconstruct the score from memory if the original were lost.

A public rehearsal of the symphony was given one day in May in the Small Hall of the Conservatory. The composer spoke to a hall filled to overflowing. He said that in the Fourteenth Symphony he was taking issue with the view that death was a release from earthly burdens and a transition to a "better world."

Let's recall, for example, the death of Boris Godunov. When Boris dies the music in some way begins to brighten. Remember Verdi's *Otello*: when the whole tragedy ends and Desdemona and Otello are dead, a wonderful tranquillity makes itself felt. Or *Aïda*, where the tragic deaths of the hero and heroine are illuminated by such radiant music. It seems that this is also the approach of our contemporaries, as witness the outstanding British composer Benjamin Britten in his *War Requiem*.

All this must stem from religious doctrines at variance with those which maintain that life is perhaps bad, but that when you die all will be well and complete tranquillity awaits you.

I think that in my Symphony I'm following in the footsteps of the great Moussorgsky. His cycle *Songs and Dances of Death*—perhaps not all of it, but certainly *The Field Marshal*—is a great protest against death, a reminder that one must live one's life honestly, nobly, honorably, never committing evil acts.

The spring months flew by quickly and summer began. On July 1 the Shostakoviches flew to Yerevan. From there they drove along the highway past the famous Lake Sevan, the jewel of Armenia, to the retreat at Dilizhan which they had come to love. He was expected: their favorite cottage, already known locally as "Shostakovich's cottage," had been made ready for them. The countryside and the quiet helped him to concentrate and to absorb himself completely in his work. That summer he orchestrated Schumann's Cello Concerto.

In his spare time he liked to meet Armenian composers staying at the retreat—there were many young people among them. They were delighted to show him their new compositions and to share artistic ideas with him. Shostakovich's replies were as usual brief, but they always provided ample food for thought, and his audience listened avidly, devouring every word.

Walking at Dilizhan was not easy for Shostakovich. The retreat was perched on the side of a mountain and there were almost no straight paths on its premises. Mountains towered all around. It was difficult there for anyone with a weak heart; not without reason had his doctors recommended that he not go to Armenia, believing that the mountain climate was bad for him. But he had gone anyway and did not regret it. His mood underwent frequent changes, like the weather so typical of those parts. A bright, deep-blue sky would suddenly be obscured by dark thunderclouds, lightning would flash, and there would be peals of thunder, always especially booming and resonant in the mountains. During a storm Shostakovich loved to stand on the balcony, as if at one with the elements. Only when the first rays of bright sunlight returned would he go back into the cottage.

This time the composer spent twenty days in all at Dilizhan. Then there was a week in Moscow, and after that a trip to Lake Baikal—one of the most arresting experiences of his later years. He decided to go by train to the lake, which was far to the east. Being in no hurry, he wanted to see as much as possible en route. The train went through places he had never visited. In the course of more than three days, a large part of the huge country passed by the windows: the picturesque countryside around Moscow, the landscapes of the Volga region, the bleak Northern Urals, the endless Siberian *taiga* and its broad rivers. But all this diversity paled before the majestic beauty of the unique fresh-water sea of Baikal.

Baikal is the only lake of its kind. The deepest in the entire world, it is distinguished by its amazingly translucent water, its unparalleled fauna, and the uniqueness of its landscape. It is surrounded by forbidding mountains from which numerous small rivers and streams flow down into the lake. Only one river has its origin in Baikal—the deep and beautiful Angara.

From the lakeside Listvinnichny Sanatorium where the Shostakoviches were staying, the composer sent enthusiastic letters describing the marvels of the region and telling his correspondents to make a point of visiting Baikal. He had a good rest at Listvinnichny, but before going back to Moscow he decided to get to know the region better, since for many years his grandparents had lived not far away in Irkutsk.

The composer's father, Dmitri Boleslavovich, was by no means a native of St. Petersburg. He had arrived in the capital at the end of the nineteenth century to obtain an education, while his parents remained far away in Siberia. The composer's grandfather, Boleslav Shostakovich, Polish by origin, was a revolutionary who had struggled against the Tsarist autocracy and been exiled to Siberia for revolutionary activity. His wife, Varvara Gavrilovna, had followed him into exile of her own free will, and they had lived in Siberia for thirty years. Children were born, grew up, and became independent. Only in 1898 was Boleslav Shostakovich able to go to St. Petersburg to visit his son Dmitri, who was studying there at the university.

At the age of 14 Shostakovich's future father had traveled to Irkutsk to see his parents and stay for their golden wedding anniversary. On the return journey a telegram reached him announcing the death of his mother. Four or five years later his father Boleslav Shostakovich was also dead, slain by the White Guard, which was fighting against the new regime. His children continued to live in Irkutsk.

Shostakovich walked round the old Siberian city, exploring it with interest. Then, after getting to know Irkutsk, he visited Ulan-Ude, capital of the Buryat Autonomous Republic, where he met composers and listened to the national music. Finally he returned to Moscow by train; its rhythmical motion did not tire him and he was able to travel comfortably and peacefully.

It had turned out to be a successful year. Admittedly it both began and ended in the hospital, but Shostakovich had long since been obliged to get used to that, and he had experienced much that was worth while: apart from interesting journeys, there had been splendid concerts including guest appearances by von Karajan; the première of the Violin Sonata in Moscow and, at the end of the year, its first Leningrad performance; successful appearances by his son (Maxim had conducted Mahler's Second Symphony); and of course the knowledge that he had written an important work: the Fourteenth Symphony, which received its première at the end of October in the hall of the Leningrad Capella Academica.

[1970-1971]

The year 1970 began with great activity. On January 4 one of Shostakovich's most tormented works, the Eighth Symphony, was performed. Then came brief trips to Leningrad to consult with Kozintsev—Shostakovich had written music for the film *King Lear*. Shostakovich was anxious to carry on at the old intense pace, but at the end of February he had to fly to the distant city of Kurgan to see Dr. Ilizarov, a well-known physician who had developed a method for treating the illness from which Shostakovich was suffering. He spent more than three months at Dr. Ilizarov's hospital, from the end of February until June 9.

Certainly the period was not wasted: he wrote the Thirteenth Quartet, similar in structure to the recently composed symphony. "I've now been in Kurgan a rather long time, undergoing treatment with the noted Dr. Ilizarov," Shostakovich wrote one of his foreign colleagues on May 2. "He's trying to fix my arms and legs." Two months later he announced that the treatment had been very helpful: "I'm going to Kurgan again around mid-August, to 'put the final chord' to the treatment, as Ilizarov says."

Contrary to his established habits, he was obliged to spend almost the whole summer in Moscow, where the regular Tchaikovsky Competition, over which Shostakovich traditionally presided, was being held. This had been the practice since the memorable first Competition, held in 1958, at which Shostakovich had ceremonially conferred the medal on the victor, a previously unknown young man from the United States named Van Cliburn.

Later Shostakovich went again to Kurgan for a stay of more than two months. Irina lived with him in the hospital. They celebrated his birthday together in modest fashion. He did not return to Moscow until early November.

The year 1970 brought a lot of creative activity. Apart from a quartet and the music for *King Lear*, there was a song cycle, *Loyalty*, consisting of settings of poems by Yevgeni Dolmatovsky for an a capella choir of male voices, and an orchestral version of a wartime opus, the six songs to verses by English poets, which he dedicated to friends.

The following year, 1971, saw the composition of the last of his symphonies, the Fifteenth—the summation of the creative career of a great symphonist of our time. It is in many ways a remarkable summing-up. After two programmatic symphonies steeped in major historical events and two symphonic song cycles in which, not content with a brief program, he made use of poems as texts, Shostakovich returned in his last symphony to a purely instrumental medium in which to embody his ideas.

Written at Repino in July 1971, the Fifteenth Symphony is notable for its strict classicism, clarity, and balance. It is a generalization of all the composer had said in his previous symphonic works, a philosophically enlightened generalization executed within a sublime scheme. It expresses eternal and unchanging values and what is innermost and deeply personal. One of the composer's letters contains the following significant observation: "I've finished another symphony —my Fifteenth. Perhaps I'll stop composing. Yet without composition I can't live."

Once he had completed the symphony Shostakovich hurried to Moscow: his son was to give the first performance.

Before him were the rehearsals, the intense activity of giving concrete form to what had hitherto been heard only in the mind of the artist. But his immediate plans remained unfulfilled. On September 16 he felt unwell during the night and was taken to the hospital. On the 18th, a week before his sixty-fifth birthday, the doctors diagnosed a second heart attack.

Until then it had seemed to Shostakovich that all was going well and he could follow his old pattern, if not at the former pace at least profitably, realizing new artistic schemes, participating actively in society, and taking interesting trips. But he was soon forced to recognize that this was no longer possible.

At first Shostakovich tried to maintain his usual routine: he went to concerts and plays, and traveled to Leningrad to take part in the rehearsals of the Fifteenth Symphony. Yevgeni Mravinsky was preparing the work with his Leningrad Philharmonic. Both in Moscow and Leningrad Shostakovich had meetings with colleagues. Shostakovich was always attentive to his fellow musicians and tried to give them help and support. This had been his practice even in his days at the Conservatory, when he would play his fellow students' compositions if they were ill, or if their own piano technique was inadequate.

Later, when he had become a prominent musician, they always turned to him in the knowledge that he would not refuse them help. He took a fatherly interest, for example, in his assistant Israel Finkelstein, helping him with his duties at the Conservatory in 1939–41. In the difficult months of the war he enabled Finkelstein to obtain warm clothing for his children, and many years later was still taking an interest in his affairs, always glad to be of assistance.

A typical incident occurred in 1962 during the second

Tchaikovsky Competition. Finkelstein had come to Moscow on his own private business and encountered Shostakovich by chance in the street. Asked what he was about, Finkelstein said he wanted to show his new piece to Sveshnikov, conductor of one of the country's finest choral groups. "Very difficult, very difficult," replied Shostakovich in his usual brisk fashion, although Finkelstein had not asked him to do anything. "Sveshnikov is Chairman of the Competition jury" (Shostakovich himself was Chairman of the organizing committee) "and he's very busy right now. I'll tell you what, call me tomorrow at 7:30 in the morning." They parted. Finkelstein telephoned punctually at 7:30 the following morning. A woman's voice answered, telling him that Shostakovich was not at home but that he had left a note: Sveshnikov would be expecting him at 4:30 that afternoon.

Some years before this episode, a book about one of the most revered of Soviet composers, Andrei Pashchenko, had appeared. In 1963, on the eve of the fiftieth anniversary of Pashchenko's distinguished artistic career, the book's author wrote Shostakovich a letter in which he said that the occasion should not pass unacknowledged: a public performance of the composer's works should be organized. "For Pashchenko this would be a well-merited reward for his many years of work, while for many composers it would be a worthwhile token of respect for a senior professional colleague." Shostakovich was quick to reply: "I have great respect for A. F. Pashchenko and his music. I think the Soviet Composers' Union has a duty to acknowledge his outstanding work. I hope that all this will be arranged satisfactorily."

The celebration did in fact take place and Shostakovich took a very active interest in its preparations. He also helped arrange for the Moscow performance of one of the symphonies of Orest Yevlakhov and of works by many other Leningrad composers.

Actively interested in his colleagues' work, Shostakovich was always warm in his approval of music he considered valuable and was quick to praise it. In 1969, when he was in the hospital and, as always, listening to music broadcasts, he made the acquaintance of a new piece by Arutyunian. He promptly sent the composer a letter:

Dear Alexander Grigorievich,

At 10:45 today (November 22nd) the radio broadcast your Sinfonietta for Chamber Orchestra.

I liked the work enormously. It was remarkably clear and skillful, with memorable themes. Everything sounded excellent. It seemed both simple and at the same time inventive and interesting.

I cannot express my admiration in writing (nor in speech, for that matter). One thing I can say: I liked your Sinfonietta very, very much.

I wish you good health and further major artistic successes. I clasp your hand firmly.

Yours,
D. Shostakovich.

A similar impulse led to the letter to Rabinovich regarding his performance of Mahler's Third Symphony, and to many other written and verbal expressions of his views.

His attentiveness to those around him, his concern for them, showed itself in everything, even in minor details that could sometimes be very touching or even comic. Once Vladislav Uspensky, one of Shostakovich's Leningrad pupils, intended to go to Moscow and wanted to see his teacher, then living at Zhukovka. He wrote the composer about this and received an immediate invitation to the dacha. The reply also contained a complete round-the-clock timetable of the train service to Zhukovka. "I was very touched by his concern that I not waste time telephoning for information or waiting in the station," Uspensky recalls. "But this wasn't an isolated instance—it was very typical of my dear teacher."

He had a similarly solicitous approach with regard to strangers, to unknown people who came to him with some request. David Oistrakh used to recount an incident which came to his knowledge when he was on tour in Odessa. A violinist in the Odessa Philharmonic Orchestra overheard her three-year-old son picking out some kind of tune on the piano. She wrote this "composition" down and sent it to Shostakovich in Moscow with the secret hope that he would detect in it signs of a gift for composition. A few days later she received a detailed reply from Shostakovich containing thoughtful educational guidance. Oistrakh read the letter. "I don't know if the little boy's opus made an impression on Shostakovich," said the violinist, "but his letter was full of sincere warmth and deep consideration for the mother's feelings, and genuinely moved me. Although tremendously busy with composition and public duties, he had found time to sit down and write a letter showing real concern to help a mother understand her son's vocation."

Reflecting on Shostakovich after his death, the composer Rodion Shchedrin wrote:

> Shostakovich was a great musician. But he was also a great human being, in that for him the practice of art and the practice of life were inseparable. When I think how one might adequately sum up his human aspect, two words come to mind: duty and conscience. Dmitri's willingness to oblige, his responsiveness and punctiliousness were truly unparalleled. In the course of his life he did so much good, helped so many people at difficult moments in their lives; many people are obliged to him for support, friendly advice, and guidance!

Many remember Shostakovich's responsiveness, the attention he paid to people. Does this imply that he was an "open" person, easygoing in his relationships? Shostakovich's nephew Dmitri Frederiks, one of those who knew him most intimately, gives this opinion: "I don't think anyone could get to know him completely. He knew how to get on with people in such a way that it seemed he was opening up to them totally. This is why a lot of people now think they were among his close friends. However, perhaps the only person who was truly close—whom Shostakovich really allowed to know him—was Ivan Sollertinsky. After Sollertinsky died two other people were quite close to him, but not to the same extent. With other acquaintances—friends and so forth—he always 'kept hidden the secrets of his heart' and so seemed different from what he really was." The most perceptive of those who came into contact with him were certainly aware of this.

In her memoirs the writer Galina Serebryakova described the impression Shostakovich had made on her long before:

As a young man Shostakovich seemed to me all the more enigmatic in that outwardly he revealed nothing of the wealth of his inner life. Certainly I realized how concentrated he was within himself, and was conscious of that strange alienation inherent in everyone totally absorbed by one aim, one idea, one passion. Creation and fanaticism, apparently so distinct, are in some way fused, just as composing and pure mathematics are inseparable. . . .

Shostakovich seemed to live largely in the world of his own deeply hidden feelings and anxious searchings. There was no trace of vanity in him. At that time his frail body was exhausted by an uncontrollable creative tension and a thirst for great achievements. Such natures are never satisfied, and to the utmost of their intellectual capacities they strive toward the impossible. As sensitive as the needle of a barometer, they suffer more keenly than others and become, as it were, the conscience of their time and place. . . . Whatever heights they attain, the higher they climb, the humbler they become. Only those who demand a great deal of themselves are truly modest and unpretentious.

On first meeting Shostakovich, the well-known pianist and teacher Alexander Goldenweiser, head of one of the schools of Soviet piano-playing, wrote in his diary: "November 25, 1943. . . . Shostakovich arrived at 5:30. He is an intelligent and uncommon man. Not very open, but certainly someone of significance."

The important phrase here is "not very open." The friends who remained closest to Shostakovich until the end of his life, Isaac Glikman, defined the fundamental characteristic of the great composer in these terms:

> . . . reserve, a striking capacity for self control, was the secret of his character, which was by nature easily roused and even irascible. . . . Shostakovich's reserve certainly had nothing in common with prudence or excessive mildness, with coldness or a sanctimonious expression. Not at all! It was a sign of enormous strength of character. That's why I very seldom had to listen to complaints from him. Complaints would have seemed inevitable in certain extremely difficult situations, but I waited in vain for a stream of bitter or indignant words. As a rule, his response to any pain caused him was a terse, superficially impassive, seemingly insignificant phrase, or most often silence. Indeed, the ancient Romans had a wise saying: "Silence cries out!" . . .
>
> Shostakovich never entered into disputes with his critics, whether serious or dull-witted, shortsighted or ill-intentioned (and there was no shortage of the latter!); he did not attempt to prove his own artistic case to them (time, the severest of judges, was later to uphold him). He was saved from such temptations not only by a feeling of his own dignity but also and principally by his reserve. . . .
>
> To his relations with people Shostakovich brought good

will, respect, and a charming lack of affectation. The noble sublimity of his spirit could always be discerned behind his reticence.

In Moscow and Leningrad, in Dilizhan, Repino, Barvikha —everywhere he spent even a few days, he seemed to be surrounded by people. Musicians, poets, and artists all sought to meet him, to enrich themselves through contact with an outstanding personality, and to convey to him some token of their respect. And it was not just the young people like the poet Yevgeni Yevtushenko and the writer Chingiz Aitmatov (whose works Shostakovich valued very highly, and with whom his acquaintance ripened into a sincere friendship, regardless of the difference in age). By no means. Shortly before her death Anna Akhmatova, Russia's most distinguished poet, came to see Shostakovich at Repino.

Akhmatova had made an impression on Shostakovich even in his childhood when, a small boy in a blue sailor suit, he had visited the home of the surgeon Grekov. He saw her there—young yet already famous. In those years, so difficult for Russia, when many artists were leaving their native land, Anna Akhmatova wrote:

> I heard a voice. Consolingly it called
> And said: go hence,
> Leave your country, backward, wicked,
> Leave Russia forever . . .
>
> Yet calmly and indifferently
> With my hands I stopped my ears,
> Lest such unworthy speech
> Profane my spirit's grief.

Akhmatova remembered the impressionable boy. Time passed; she became aware of his fame and was attracted by his music. The war had already receded far into the past, yet Akhmatova could still recall the dreadful days when she, like

Shostakovich, had been rescued by air from besieged Leningrad:

> You would all have admired me
> When in the belly of a flying fish
> I fled from savage pursuit,
> Flying by night over Lake Ladoga
> And the forest, like one possessed by the devil
> Hurrying to the Brocken . . .
>
> Behind me, gleaming mysteriously
> And calling itself "The Seventh,"
> Hastening to the feast of the unheard,
> Locked in a manuscript book,
> The famous *Leningrad* Symphony
> Was returning to its native air.

So they met. It is not known what they talked about on this occasion. They may have listened to his music, or perhaps to her poems. But in 1973 Shostakovich concluded a song cycle to poems by Marina Tsvetaeva with a section dedicated to Akhmatova.

[1972–1974]

In mid-1972 the composer spent over a month in the German Democratic Republic, staying in Berlin and Dresden. He looked over the medieval fortress at Königstein, then visited West Berlin, where the U.S.S.R. State Symphony Orchestra played the Fifteenth Symphony under the direction of Yevgeni Svetlanov.

He returned briefly to Moscow, and after two weeks' rest set off from Leningrad to London on the liner *Baltica*. The ultimate destination of his journey was the Republic of Ireland, and he flew there the day the ship docked. At a ceremony in Trinity College, Dublin, the honorary degree of Doctor of Music was conferred on him.

This was by no means the first honorary degree the composer had received outside his country. Almost twenty years before, in 1954, he had been made an honorary member of the Swedish Royal Academy. Subsequently he had been elected a corresponding member of the Academy of Arts of the German Democratic Republic, and an honorary member of the Santa Cecilia Academy of Arts in Italy. In 1958 he had received several flattering signs of international recognition: he became a member of the British Royal Academy of Music, an honorary Doctor of Music at Oxford University, Commander of the French Order of Arts and Letters, winner of the International Jan Sibelius Prize and, a few months later, Professor of the Mexican Conservatory and a member of the American Academy of Sciences.

From 1966 to 1972 Shostakovich received the Gold Medal of the British Royal Philharmonic Society, the Order of the Great Silver Medal of Honor (for his services to the Austrian Republic), the Mozart Memorial Medal awarded by the governors of the Mozart Society in Vienna, and the Great Star of the Friendship of Peoples medal awarded by the German Democratic Republic. He also became a corresponding member of the Bavarian Academy of Fine Arts and an honorary member of the Finnish Association of Composers.

In the summer of 1972, on the way back from Dublin Shostakovich stopped off in England. He went to the British Museum and the Royal Opera House at Covent Garden, and heard Mass in St. Paul's Cathedral. Then he traveled with Britten to Aldeburgh, the small town by the sea where the English composer had chosen to live.

He returned to Russia again on board the *Baltica*, and spent more than a month relaxing at the dacha. In the fall, after a period of rest in a sanatorium, he again set off for England, this time by air: he had promised the Fitzwilliam Quartet, an ensemble of young musicians, that he would be present at the British première of the Thirteenth Quartet, to be given at York University.

He was met at York railway station by one of the Quartet's members. Suspecting how difficult it would be for the young musicians to play in his presence for the first time, and not wishing to complicate the première for them, Shostakovich suggested that he listen to them in rehearsal before the concert began. The members of the Quartet were deeply touched by his concern for their peace of mind at the concert, and by the sacrifice of his own plans and time.

The evening concert at the university became a true cele-

bration. "The presence of the composer excited the audience
—everyone there felt he was present at a great event," recalled the violist Alan George.

> For his part, Shostakovich was visibly moved by the recep-
> tion given him by the public: although inured to expressions
> of enthusiasm, he nonetheless took the ovation as though it
> were the first he had received in his life.
>
> The following morning Shostakovich invited us to his hotel
> and we played for him again. It is difficult to express how
> valuable these hours were for us: as we played for the com-
> poser we could see his face and we were in the most vital and
> direct contact with him. Later we accompanied him to the
> station, and he waved to us with his ailing hand until the
> train disappeared from view.

In London, where a festival of Russian music was in
progress, the Fifteenth Symphony was performed with
Maxim Shostakovich as conductor. Once again there were
ovations, and once again a capacity audience went into rap-
tures over this brilliant music and welcomed its creator
warmly. After several days packed with concerts, plays, and
official meetings, Shostakovich flew to Moscow. Soon after
his arrival he was taken to the hospital with renal colic.
Examinations revealed a dark patch on the left lung; it was a
malignant tumor.

For the first time in ten years Shostakovich did not greet
the new year at home in the family surroundings that meant
so much to him. Not until February did he leave the hospital after a course of radiation therapy, and he was out for
only a month, since the treatment had to be repeated in
March. But he did manage to make good use of the time
available to him, going once again to Berlin, where both his
operas were being staged. He took part in rehearsals of
Katerina Izmailova, stayed to see the première, watched a

production of *The Nose*, and as usual went to other plays and concerts and gave a press conference.

After the hospital came Repino.

The authors often used to meet Shostakovich there. Somehow we would be in the same places that he was during the same months—in the early, tentative Leningrad spring or in the fall, in October.

We would encounter him moving slowly along the paths and avenues, or in front of the little house in which so many of his greatest works had been composed. He made a surprising impression on us at that time. Elderly and suffering from numerous illnesses, he seemed intensely concentrated upon something known only to himself. It seemed as if he carried within him music which he alone could hear, and that this was why he walked so slowly and cautiously, as if afraid it would evaporate before he grasped it. We decided not to go up to him and start a conversation which would distract him from the music that was almost audible when one looked at him. Only later did we learn that he had been aware of his approaching end, and that he was indeed in a hurry to express everything within him that required utterance.

All the things a person usually takes for granted were difficult for him: going to the dining room, going up the steps, shaking hands, sitting down, standing up.

This time when Israel Finkelstein came, he wanted to show him a new composition, a cello sonata. Finkelstein lived in Leningrad, but arrived one day in Repino. Literally within minutes the telephone in his chalet rang. It was Shostakovich: "I know you're here, so come on over. But bring someone with you—I can't turn the pages. Once I stand up, I can't sit down again."

Even so he continued to meet colleagues, to listen to their music and to talk. In his spare time he would go out for some exercise, supported under the arm by his wife. But for the most part he worked. Illuminated by a table lamp, the silhouette of the composer bent over his writing table could be seen in the window of the little chalet in the morning, the afternoon, and late in the evening. He was writing his Fourteenth Quartet.

In early May, however, the Shostakoviches started out on their most extended journey, flying first to Copenhagen. What drew Shostakovich to Denmark was what brought him to the vast majority of other countries: a production of *Katerina Izmailova*. Unlike the other trips, however, on this occasion the composer was in no hurry to return home. After some days in Copenhagen Shostakovich moved to a small, isolated boarding house on the shores of a lake, by way of a break from the rehearsals of the opera. The composer rested and walked in the woods by the shore. Irina hired a car and they drove around the district and went to the seaside. They managed to have ten peaceful days of totally unclouded relaxation.

Another week in Copenhagen followed: Maxim was conducting the Fifteenth Symphony. Then on June 2 Shostakovich and his wife flew to Paris and by the next day reached Le Havre, where they embarked on the liner *Mikhail Lermontov*, en route from Leningrad to New York. The week at sea was peaceful and the weather bright and fine. The ship scarcely rolled—not that Shostakovich was afraid of rough seas; on the contrary, they delighted him.

The doctors in Moscow had tried to make Shostakovich give up the journey, warning him that he might not be strong enough to withstand it. Nevertheless he had wanted to go very much. Northwestern University was to confer on him the degree of Honorary Doctor. The composer also wanted to pay one more visit—his last—to the Western Hemisphere and to see as much as he could of the United States, that vast country about which he felt he did not know nearly enough.

His family had other reasons for wanting him to go: it was their last hope. The Moscow doctors did not hide from them the gravity of his state of health, expecially now that in addition to heart disease and an illness of the nervous system he had a tumor very close to the aorta; they believed that the time had come when medicine was powerless. This had been the opinion of the most prominent and authoritative doctors. There was no reason to disbelieve them, but it is human nature to hope, so Irina had decided to seek the advice of the most eminent American specialists.

The days on the liner flowed by unhurriedly and the weather stayed fine; the composer enjoyed the voyage as for more than a week the *Mikhail Lermontov* sailed across the Atlantic. They arrived in New York on June 11, spent three days there, and then set off for Evanston, Illinois. They went by train, a journey that from New York took almost twenty-four hours: as always the composer wanted to see as much as possible. He sat at the window of the train gazing with curiosity at the landscapes rushing by, until it grew so dark that only lights could be seen.

In Evanston the honorary degree of Doctor of Fine Arts was conferred on Shostakovich. After this came two painful days in a Washington hospital, where the composer was given a thorough medical examination. The American doctors had nothing new to relate. Their diagnosis and prognosis were identical to those given by the experts in Moscow. There could be no more grounds for hope.

Shostakovich returned to Europe on the liner *Queen Elizabeth*. On June 26 the coast of England rose from the horizon in a dull haze. Next day he took the first flight back to Moscow.

He had no desire to travel anywhere after a journey which

for a sick man had been so extensive and so exhausting. July he spent resting at the dacha. Staying on the Baltic coast in August, he wrote a song cycle to poems by Marina Tsvetaeva called *Six Poems of Marina Tsvetaeva for Contralto and Piano.* The titles of the songs are *To My Verses, Whence This Tenderness, Hamlet's Dialogue with His Conscience, The Poet and the Emperor, Not a Drum Was Heard. . . ,* and *To Anna Akhmatova.* In content and form they differ widely, but clearly linking the cycle is the theme of creation and the creator, the role, significance, and high calling of the singer/poet. Tsvetaeva herself, Pushkin, and Anna Akhmatova are the heroes of the poems; the composer celebrates them, reflecting at the same time on himself and his own work.

On August 30 Shostakovich returned to Moscow. Rehearsals of the Fourteenth Quartet were commencing and, as always, the composer wanted to take a most active part in them.

Wrote Dmitri Tsyganov:

> In the reminiscences of musicians who came into contact with Shostakovich in the course of preparations for a performance of his works, one often finds mention of the extreme delicacy of the composer's observations. I could give a host of such examples from the experience of our Quartet, and more than that, I could tell you that the composer was always ready to assume responsibility for passages which through our fault did not at first succeed ("This evidently didn't work out for me").
>
> Most surprising, however, was something else. Behind the gentleness and unobtrusiveness of Shostakovich's observations lay a profound sense of conviction concerning everything which touched upon the problems of interpreting his works.
>
> Could it indeed have been otherwise? He did not need the rehearsal process in order to check, still less to alter, any

details of the new work. (An artist of true genius, Shostakovich put down on paper his creative ideas only when they
had finally crystalized in his mind.) He needed rehearsals in
order to bring the musicians nearer to his vision of the way
the music should sound. Thus he never found rehearsals a
burdensome obligation. On the contrary, Shostakovich once
acknowledged that he derived the greatest pleasure from preparing for the première of a new work, since the first performance itself was merely the outcome of that process.
Those lucky enough to have been present at the rehearsals
of Shostakovich's last quartets could see how the gravely or
rather hopelessly ill composer was transformed: he came to
life, his eyes blazed, and all his ailments vanished for a
while.

One of the lucky ones was the writer Chingiz Aitmatov.
He arrived in Moscow and was, as always, more than happy
to meet Shostakovich. The composer invited him to dinner
and told him that before they ate he would hear his new
composition—the Fourteenth Quartet. The performance
would begin punctually at seven o'clock.

Aitmatov was unable to get there by seven, having been
delayed at the editorial office. At 7:10 he was at the door of
Shostakovich's apartment; the sounds of music reached him.

Treading noiselessly in order not to disturb the composer, I
sat down on the sofa just beside the door. No one even
glanced at me. The musicians were playing and Shostakovich, his head buried in his own score, and Kara Karaev,
leaning forward, were listening intently. They listened as if
something extraordinary were about to occur, as if they were
keenly following some invisible event which I couldn't see,
but they could. . . .

    . . . Shostakovich listened to the playing throughout with
the same fierce, unremitting attention, as if anxious to isolate,
to identify, something in the musical sounds he hadn't quite
succeeded in expressing, hadn't quite found. From the side

his face seemed somehow remote, unfamiliar and even stern, inaccessible. With bewilderment and alarm I looked at his back, bent over and rigid, and the severe aspect of his half-turned face. My premonition had not deceived me. When the musicians at last stopped playing, Shostakovich didn't immediately relax his tense aquiline posture, although Kara Karaev, feeling genuine admiration and expressing the emotion he had just experienced while trying to maintain a restrained and everyday tone of voice, said at once,

"Dmitri, it's a work of genius!" and thanked the performers warmly.

Shostakovich, however, remained aloof, although he nodded in gratitude. I didn't recognize him. Some kind of mercilessly exacting force had awakened in him, a force which exerted itself both on himself and others. To begin with, he too thanked the musicians. Then he launched upon a severe critique of the performance. Kara Karaev even felt obliged to soften the tone of the composer's remarks. Heaven knows, the musicians had played excellently, not merely with intelligence and feeling, but giving their whole being to the music they were performing, just as race horses force themselves to a relentless gallop when their strength is at its last gasp. But the composer demanded more skill, more precision, more inspiration. He even complained to one of the players that he was breathing too audibly as he moved his bow. He had been associated with this Quartet for years—more than thirty years of artistic collaboration. Yet how strict he was with them! For a long time the composer and performers continued to discuss and dispute, now agreeing, now differing in their views. This was a true dialogue between the creators of music. And Shostakovich's composition was indeed worthy of this labor and this unconditionally responsible approach to art.

Later they decided to play through the Fourteenth Quartet once more. I listened and marveled: So that's the kind of man you are! Gentle, good-hearted, diffident Shostakovich—but a wild beast when it comes to work!

This exactingness, of course, is explained by the thirty years of work the composer had shared with the performers. He was confident of their complete understanding and knew he could ask from them a perfect realization of his ideas. That was far from the case with all musicians. On other occasions he made no comments at all—and not because there were none to make. He simply knew it would be of no help. There were performances of his works which he preferred not to attend.

"When father had faith in a perfomer he would take a most active part in the creative process," said Maxim Shostakovich. "If on the other hand he didn't believe in someone, if he understood that any interference would be in vain, somehow he immediately shut himself off, and in reply to the musician's query about his performance would usually say hastily, 'Fine, fine.' Those he trusted and liked would sometimes be told their performance had been bad."

Shostakovich's remarkable and "absolute" punctuality, another aspect of his personality, is illustrated by Chingiz Aitmatov's story just recounted. "Father looked on time as something of the highest value," Maxim Shostakovich explains. "And if he was ever invited to, say, the Ministry of Culture for an appointment at 4:30, you could have set your watch by him. At precisely 4:30 he would be where he was expected. Not at twenty-nine minutes past the hour, but at 4:30 exactly."

Shostakovich never put anyone in the position of having to wait for him: he was extremely careful about time, his own and other people's. This is probably the reason why he was able to find time to accomplish such a remarkable, indeed fantastic, amount—and perhaps too why he had a rather special attitude toward clocks. At home he had lots of them, big, ancient grandfather clocks, wall clocks, table clocks. He himself saw to it that they all kept time and that they all began to strike at exactly the same moment—as they did, inexorably, counting out the last months of his life.

November saw the première of the Fourteenth Quartet. It was a notable concert: the Beethoven Quartet, Shostakovich's favorite musical ensemble, had recently celebrated a half-century of playing. Over the years the personnel of the group had changed: the violinist Vasili Shirinsky and the viola player Borisovsky had died. But the young musicians who took their places, Zabavnikov and Druzhinin, merged naturally into the ensemble. Now there was a new Shostakovich quartet for them to perform, dedicated to one of the group's members, the cellist Sergei Shirinsky.

The dedication is underlined by the music: the cello quotes a line from *Katerina Izmailova*, the melody accompanying the words "Seryozha, my dear one!" In the finale a theme appears which uses the notes that in German notation make up the name "Sergei," of which "Seryozha" is a diminutive form. Shirinsky said with emotion: "This music has graced half my life. I feel I haven't lived in vain."

Unfortunately, his days too were numbered. The Beethoven Quartet was unable to give the première of Shostakovich's next composition, the Fifteenth Quartet, because Sergei Shirinsky had died while rehearsals of that quartet were underway. The ensemble was orphaned, and time was needed to find a replacement for the cellist it had lost, one who could blend into the group and become a true "Beethovener." The première was entrusted instead to the Taneev Quartet of Leningrad.

The Fifteenth Quartet, composed at Repino in July 1974, is an astonishing work, the only one of its kind. It consists of six slow movements following without a break, all in E flat minor. Despite the music's uniformity of development and its length, the quartet does not give the impression of being overextended.

Shostakovich was writing about a subject that wholly pre-occupied him at the time and of thoughts which obsessed him: the meaning of life and its end; death and immortality; the role of the artist and his work; himself. The writing is nervous, passionate, and tormented. This theme was so close to him and so engrossed him that he continued to reflect on it after completing the quartet. It still needed concrete form.

Returning from Repino to his dacha near Moscow, Sho-stakovich embarked on his next opus. He had come across a recently published volume of the poems of Michelangelo Buonarroti in translations by Efros, the noted Soviet literary scholar. In the poems of this towering Renaissance figure, Shostakovich found thoughts and feelings akin to his own, and he conceived the idea of setting them to music.

Shostakovich selected eleven poems, to which he gave the titles *Truth, Morning, Love, Separation, Anger, Dante, The Exile, Creation, Night, Death*, and *Immortality*. The transla-tions were not the work of a professional poet and did not altogether suit him, so he asked Andrei Voznesensky to ex-amine them and make corrections, although he was not seek-ing new versions: such was his preoccupation with his sub-ject. Soon the work was completed. Disliking the term "cycle," the composer entitled it *Suite for Bass Voice and Piano to Poems by Michelangelo Buonarroti* and dedicated it to his wife Irina.

The content of the *Suite* turned out to be broader in range than that of the quartet. Apart from reflections on life and death and an affirmation of the artist's destiny on earth, the work contains meditations on love and the beloved, and per-haps a farewell to her—a farewell anticipating an inevitable and by now imminent separation.

He was anxious to hear what he had written as soon as possible. Two superb musicians were to perform it—the magnificent bass Yevgeni Nesterenko and his accompanist,

Yevgeni Shenderovich. Shostakovich had already given them the score when Voznesensky brought his translation. It was very good, clearer and more interesting than the one the composer had been using. He accepted the poems gratefully, then realized he could not use them. He had created the music to fit the lines of the original translation; they had fused into a single entity, and it proved impossible to eliminate or replace anything. He apologized in dismay to the poet and awaited the première. It was postponed on account of an accident: Nesterenko broke a leg.

This was in the autumn. The composer had already returned from the dacha to take part as best he could in the preparations for the première of *The Nose*. This afforded him perhaps the greatest satisfaction of his final years. Shostakovich had long dreamed of seeing his youthful opera on the stage. He had attended a performance of *The Nose* in Berlin and thought highly of the production. He knew that the opera was being played in Czechoslovakia, and in Italy at Florence and Rome, and that the producer of both Italian versions was Eduardo de Filippo. He was very pleased by this—how could he not be?—but still longed to see a production in Russia.

Suddenly his dream was realized. After almost forty-five years, *The Nose* was resurrected. The production was mounted by the conductor Gennadi Rozhdestvensky and the director Boris Pokrovsky in the recently opened Moscow Chamber Opera Theater. Before directing the production, Pokrovsky decided to meet the composer. He had no idea what they would talk about and was astonished: totally unprepared for a conversation about *The Nose*, Shostakovich exhibited a remarkable memory and a knowledge of every bar, every note of a score he had written half a century before!

The composer was anxious to attend all the rehearsals, but

his health did not permit it. He managed to be present only at some of the last ones, listening closely and tensely, offering tactful observations—such as could be put into effect in the few remaining days. He was happy to watch his youthful creation come to life, and to see the enthusiasm with which the young singers worked on it.

The final rehearsals of *The Nose* were recorded on film. In the television film made at the time, the composer can be seen making his way with difficulty through the hall, assisted by his wife. "Dmitri was very ill," recounts the film's producer, Yuri Belyakin. "So much so that he had to be led to the location. Once the music began, however, he was transformed."

The success which greeted the première could be described as triumphant. Shostakovich felt on top of the world. Yet within a space of days two severe blows fell in rapid succession. First Sergei Shirinsky died; Shostakovich attended his funeral on October 23. Then five days later there was another funeral—David Oistrakh's. Two fine musicians had departed this life, two sensitive interpreters of Shostakovich's works who had been very much associated with him. Their burial was like the burial of part of his own life.

[1974–1975]

There had been so many of these bereavements in his life, ever since that distant wintry day when, as a boy of fifteen, he had seen his father buried. His mother and his first wife had long since died, as had his sister Maria, not to mention all the friends now gone.

Lev Oborin, an excellent musician and a good friend, had also died recently. They had got to know each other fifty years before. At that time Oborin had been sixteen years old and was studying in the fourth year at the Conservatory. A year before they had entered the Conservatory, a circle of young people had formed. Usually they met at the Oborins' and played music—Bach, Bruckner, Richard Strauss, Scriabin, and Glazounov. Passing through Moscow in the fall of 1924, Shostakovich had happened upon one of the meetings of the group, and his friendship with Oborin and Shebalin was cemented at that time. By December Oborin had come to Leningrad at Shostakovich's invitation and stayed at his apartment. Shostakovich took upon himself all the responsibility for organizing the young pianist's first Leningrad appearance.

In the years that followed, Shostakovich, who often visited Moscow, had never failed to meet Oborin, and entrusted him with the performance of his piano music. This growing friendship did not prevent the two musicians from competing against each other: both were sent to the First Chopin Competition and Oborin, as noted earlier, emerged the victor.

In subsequent years their association was close and friendly. Shostakovich was genuinely glad to have Oborin with him on the difficult and exhausting tour of Turkey, and was still more pleased when Oborin turned up in Kuibyshev during the war. Their relations were good in no merely ordinary sense. Shostakovich valued Oborin highly as a pianist and as a musician. He was one of the select few from whom Shostakovich would seek advice on matters concerning his music.

"While I was ill I composed the first movement of a piano sonata," wrote Shostakovich to Sollertinsky on February 19, 1943. "I'm starting on the second movement. So as you can see, I'm working. Lev [Oborin] praised the first movement yesterday evening and suggested I delete one superfluous page, which I did. He's a brilliant musician and immediately pointed out and corrected shortcomings which had been tormenting my conscience."

Now Oborin was no more. It was some years too since Shebalin had died—Vissarion Shebalin the composer, whose acquaintance Shostakovich had made at the same time, during the fall of 1924. Oborin and the composer had at once become friends. As early as March 1925 there had been a joint concert of their music in Moscow. In the first half, works by Shelbalin were played, while the second half had been devoted to Shostakovich. Oborin was most actively involved in the concert: he played Shebalin's *Quasi-sonata*, was one of the performers in a trio by Shostakovich, and played the latter's Suite for Two Pianos with the composer.

In the fall of 1926 Shebalin came to Leningrad, where his symphony was to be performed. Wrote Shebalin:

> It was my first acquaintance with Leningrad, which impressed me by its severity and majesty and by the beauty of its architecture. I saw the hall of the Philharmonic for the first time, too. It was in this hall that I had my orchestral

"christening." I conducted a symphony by K. S. Saradzhev.
. . . After the first rehearsal Dmitri, with whom my wife and
I were staying, helped me correct the orchestral parts. He sat
down and deleted the mistakes. . . .

The Shostakovich household, thanks to the exceptional
cordiality and hospitality of Dmitri's mother Sofia, was like
a magnet for young people and was always full of guests.

At the end of 1942 Shebalin was appointed Director of the
Moscow Conservatory. One of his first steps in his new capacity was to invite Shostakovich to become Professor of
Composition. It is striking that Shebalin, having invited Shostakovich, then turned over some of his pupils to him—first
Revol Bunin and later Karen Khachaturian—believing that
he would be a more suitable instructor for them. In their
subsequent work together, there were occasions when a student would request a transfer from Shebalin's class to Shostakovich's. Never once did this cloud the great friendship
between the two composers.

Much more could be said of their warm and sincere relationship, their work together, and the attentive and impartial
criticism each bestowed on the other's music. After Shebalin's death, Shostakovich wrote in a volume of articles dedicated to his memory: "He was an extremely fine person. I
always admired his goodness, honesty, and exceptional ad-
herence to principle. What a remarkable friend he was! How
pleasant it was to share one's joys and sorrows with him! In
his company joy became greater and grief less!"

There were others whom Shostakovich admired and with
whom he maintained close relationships—for example,
Mikhail Zoshchenko. Shostakovich regarded his gifts as a
writer highly and liked him as a person. Zoshchenko used to
stay with the Shostakovich family at his mother's hospitable
apartment on Dmitrov Lane.

Or Vladimir Lebedev. An artist, the talented and original

illustrator of numerous children's books, he was also very keen on sports, so much so that he had at one time even been a boxing referee. This common ground brought the two men together in the mid-1930s.

And Grigori Kozintsev. The director of many films for which Shostakovich had written the score, he attracted the composer by his outstanding qualities, his talent, and his idiosyncratic outlook on life. Shostakovich enjoyed working with him, but with no less pleasure maintained contact with him "unofficially"—in domestic surroundings away from work, during his free time.

All these friends were now dead. Of his contemporaries perhaps only Lev Arnshtam remained: at one time a pianist and fellow student with Shostakovich in the piano class at the Leningrad Conservatory, he had subsequently become the noted film director responsible for *Girlfriends*, *Zoya*, and *Five Days, Five Nights*, for which Shostakovich had written the music.

Younger friends of course remained. There were his colleagues, often former pupils: Yuri Sviridov, Yuri Levitin, Venyamin Basner, Boris Tishchenko. And Aram Khachaturian was still alive. This was a consolation, yet there had been so many irrecoverable losses, so many gaps which could not be filled.

The year 1974 came to an end. As always Shostakovich kept up an active life crowded with events. He attended a concert by Sviatoslav Richter in the Great Hall of the Conservatory and a full rehearsal of the ballet *Ivan the Terrible*, to music by Prokofiev, which was being staged at the Bolshoi Theater. He also took an energetic part in a recording of *The Nose*.

He went to Leningrad for a few days to be present at the anniversary concert of one of his colleagues; there he also saw two plays, met some of his former pupils, and attended a full rehearsal and the première of Weinberg's opera *Zosia*, which was being staged by the opera studio of the Leningrad Conservatory.

Meanwhile he continued with his work, making an orchestral version of the Michelangelo Suite and then, with Yevgeni Nesterenko once again in mind, wrote the humorous but somewhat eerie *Four Poems of Captain Lebyadkin* to texts from Dostoevsky's novel *The Devils*. "I think I've managed to capture the spirit of Dostoevsky in this work," said Shostakovich. "Lebyadkin is of course a buffoon, but from time to time he becomes terrifying."

Yet another work was written for Nesterenko. In January the singer approached him for advice: which composer should he ask to orchestrate Beethoven's *Song of the Flea* for a program of music inspired by Goethe's *Faust*? Shostakovich mentioned a few names and then began to think. Suddenly he said, "Let me do it— I have no work in hand just now." Very soon the score was ready.

In March, feeling in need of a rest, he went to the sanatorium in Barvikha where he had been sent after his second heart attack. It had a beneficial effect on him; by April he felt considerably better. Even his right hand, which had not been functioning for a long time, began to move again.

There was welcome news from France—Shostakovich had been elected an honorary member of the French Academy of Fine Arts. Obviously he was unable to go to Paris straightaway.

In May he decided to go to Repino. He had had a new idea which could be worked out only in the familiar creative environment so dear to him, far from the incessant bustle which distracted him from his thoughts. They arrived on May 11. The following day, as had long been his custom, they celebrated the anniversary of the première of the First

Symphony—the forty-eighth anniversary of the day which Shostakovich considered his birthday as a composer. Then he got to work—on Opus 147, which was to be the last of his compositions.

He finished the work in June, after returning to Moscow. But toward the end of the month his health deteriorated, so his doctor put him in the hospital, where he spent almost the whole of July. He was suffering from pains in the liver. Even so he continued to work, correcting the sheets of the Viola Sonata which had been brought to him from the copyist.

On July 31 the doctors met in consultation. Their melancholy conclusion was that nothing further could be done; it was just a matter of time. The next day they discharged him and he went to the dacha. A day later his condition worsened—so much so that the doctors again insisted on hospitalizing him. On August 3 Shostakovich entered the hospital for the last time. On August 8 he asked that he be wakened earlier than usual the next day: there was an interesting soccer match that he did not want to miss. But it was not to be. On the morning of August 9, 1975, Shostakovich died.

Shostakovich's stature as a composer is undisputed, but for those who knew him the influence of his personality and the austere and illustrious example he set in life are perhaps no less important.

We would therefore like to conclude our story with the words of one of Shostakovich's pupils, the composer Boris Tishchenko: "I have neither the skill, the knowledge, nor the understanding to sum up the significance of that tremendous phenomenon which we knew by the name of Shostakovich. Our generation grew up on his music and with his name on our lips. So our hearts would miss a beat when he took off his spectacles to clean them and we caught a glimpse of him, like a knight without armor, close to us, defenseless. The influence of his personality was so great that one began oneself to change, to become ashamed of one's insignificance, one's ineptitude, one's lack of understanding. That such a man lived has made the world a much finer place. We must all learn from him, and not from his music alone.

On October 1, 1975, International Music Day, the regular concert season opened in the Small Hall of the Leningrad Philharmonic. By tradition the first concert was devoted to the music of Shostakovich. It was an evening of sonatas. In the first half the Sonata for Cello and Piano was played, and also the Violin Sonata dedicated to David Oistrakh. The second half consisted of Shostakovich's last and previously unheard work, the Sonata for Viola and Piano: an astonishing piece, sublimely beautiful, it seems to have crossed the threshold dividing life and death. It shows no sign of horror, despair, or fear in the face of impending Fate; it is humane, pure, and wise.

A reverential silence reigned in a hall filled to capacity—so packed that there was no room left to stand: against the walls and in all the aisles stood those who, unable to obtain seats, could not bear to miss the concert. Only one seat was left empty, covered with bouquets of fresh flowers: the seat Shostakovich had always occupied.

Index